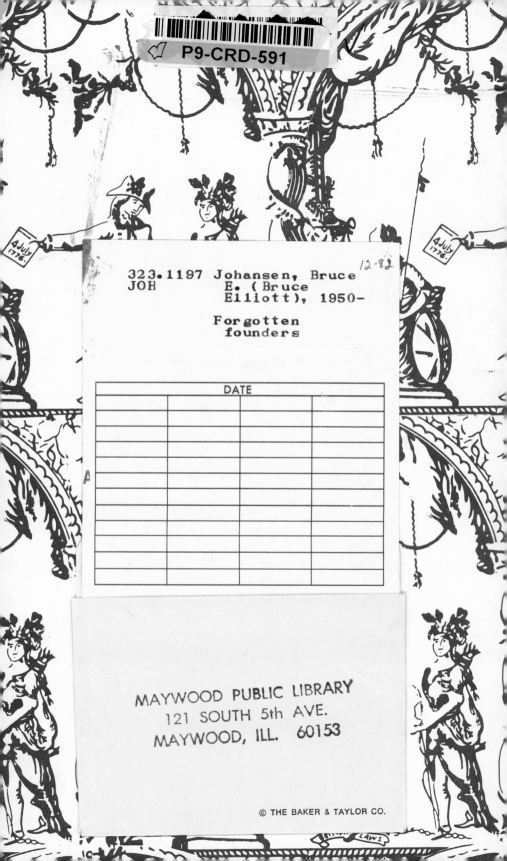

FORGOTTEN

FOUNDERS

FORGOTTEN FOUNDERS

By BRUCE E. JOHANSEN

---

*Benjamin Franklin, the Iroquois
and the Rationale for the
American Revolution*

1982

Gambit INCORPORATED, *Publishers*

OF IPSWICH, MASSACHUSETTS

First Printing

Library of Congress Cataloging in Publication Data

Johansen, Bruce E. (Bruce Elliott), 1950–
   Forgotten founders

   Bibliography
   Includes Index.
      1.   Iroquois Indians—Tribal government.   2.   Indians
of North America—Tribal government.   3.   Franklin, Benja-
min, 1706–1790.   4.   United States—Politics and govern-
ment—Colonial period, ca. 1600–1775.   5.   United States
—Politics and government—Revolution, 1775–1783.
I.   Title.
E99.I7J63   323.1'197   81-23726
ISBN 0-87645-111-3   AACR2

Printed in the United States of America.

For *my parents,*

and

for John Crazy Bear, a Seneca who breathed
life into the Iroquois' Great Law of Peace for me

CONTENTS

ACKNOWLEDGMENTS

Like most books, this one would never have been written without the encouragement, criticism, skepticism, and selfless devotion of many people. First among those people are the Indians who challenged me to find in the white man's archives documentary proof to buttress Indian oral history. Thanks go to John Crazy Bear, a Seneca whose ancestors helped make an American of Benjamin Franklin, and to Phil Lucas, who provided early help with research leads, as well as Vine Deloria, Jr., whose encouragement (not to mention his many books) helped inspire me.

Thanks go also to Sheldon Harsel, Alex Edelstein, Vernon Carstensen, and Russel Barsh, as well as William E. Ames, all of the University of Washington, who provided invaluable criticism, and who were willing to listen to ideas for which other academics might have threatened to bust me down to a B.A. and hustle me off to the nut house. Roberto F. Maestas, a Chicano Pueblo, director of Seattle's El Centro de la Raza and compadre co-author of many years, also helped provide focus to the many drafts of this book. Alvin Josephy, Jr., also deserves many thanks for his criticisms and opinions of an early draft, as does Bruce Brown.

Invaluable aid also was given by many librarians and archivists, some of whom work at the University of Washington Libraries, the New York City Public Library, the American Philosophical Society, the Library of Congress (General Collection and Manuscript Division), the Department of Interior's Library, the New-

Acknowledgments

berry Library, in Chicago, and the Smithsonian Institution's National Anthropological Archives.

Many thanks go also to my aunt and uncle, who put up this savage from the mountains of western America in a style to which he ought never to become accustomed in Washington, D.C., and to Judy Ruben, who ensured that I would stay alive on meager means on Manhattan Island, not an easy task these days.

To all of you, and to Lovell Thompson and Mark Saxton of Gambit: you wouldn't be seeing this book if it weren't for your part in making it possible.

—B.E.J.

[*x*]

INTRODUCTION

It is now time for a destructive order to be reversed, and it is well
to inform other races that the aboriginal cultures of North
America were not devoid of beauty. Futhermore, in denying the
Indian his ancestral rights and heritages the white race is but rob-
bing itself. America can be revived, rejuvenated, by recognizing a
Native School of thought.

—Chief Luther Standing Bear
Lakota (Sioux)
Land of the Spotted Eagle

The seeds for this book were sown in my mind during a late-sum-
mer day in 1975, by a young American Indian whose name I've
long since forgotten. As a reporter for the *Seattle Times*, I had
been researching a series of articles on Washington State Indian
tribes. The research took me to Evergreen State College in Olym-
pia, where a young woman, an undergraduate in the American
Indian studies program, told me in passing that the Iroquois had
played a key role in the evolution of American democracy.

The idea at first struck me as disingenuous. I considered myself
decently educated in American history, and to the best of my
knowledge, government for and by the people had been invented

[*xi*]

by white men in powdered wigs. I asked the young woman where she had come by her information.

"My grandmother told me," she said. That was hardly the kind of source one could use for a newspaper story. I asked whether she knew of any other sources. "You're the investigative reporter," she said. "You find them."

Back at the city desk, treed cats and petty crime were much more newsworthy than two-centuries-past revels in the woods the width of a continent away. For a time I forgot the meeting at Evergreen, but never completely. The woman's challenge stayed with me through another year at the *Times*, the writing of a book on American Indians, and most of a Ph.D. program at the University of Washington. I collected tantalizing shreds—a piece of a quotation from Benjamin Franklin here, an allegation there. Individually, these meant little. Together, however, they began to assume the outline of a plausible argument that the Iroquois had indeed played a key role in the ideological birth of the United States, especially through Franklin's advocacy of federal union.

Late in 1978, the time came to venture the topic for my Ph.D. dissertation in history and communications. I proposed an investigation of the role that Iroquois political and social thought had played in the thinking of Franklin and Thomas Jefferson. Members of my supervisory committee were not enthusiastic. Doubtless out of concern for my academic safety, I was advised to test my water wings a little closer to the dock of established knowledge. The professors, however, did not deny my request. Rather, I was invited to flail as far out as I might before returning to the dock, colder, wetter, and presumably wiser.

I plunged in, reading the published and unpublished papers of Franklin and Jefferson, along with all manner of revolutionary history, Iroquois ethnology, and whatever else came my way. Wandering through a maze of footnotes, I early on found an article by Felix Cohen, published in 1952. Cohen, probably the most outstanding scholar of American Indian law of his or any other age, argued the thesis I was investigating in the *American Scholar.* Like the Indian student I had encountered more than three years earlier, he seemed to be laying down the gauntlet—providing a few enticing leads (summarized here in chapter one), with no footnotes or any other documentation.

After several months of research, I found two dozen scholars who had raised the question since 1851, usually in the context of studies with other objectives. Many of them urged further study of the American Indians' (especially the Iroquois') contribution to the nation's formative ideology, particularly the ideas of federal union, public opinion in governance, political liberty, and the government's role in guaranteeing citizens' well-being—"happiness," in the eighteenth-century sense.

The most recent of these suggestions came through Donald Grinde, whose *The Iroquois and the Founding of the American Nation* (1979) reached me in the midst of my research. Grinde summarized much of what had been written to date, reserving special attention for Franklin, and then wrote that "more needs to be done, especially if America continues to view itself as a distinct entity set apart from many of the values of Western civilization." He also suggested that such a study could help dissolve negative stereotypes that many Euro-Americans still harbor toward American Indians' mental abilities and heritage.

By this time, I was past worrying whether I had a story to tell. The question was *how* to tell it: how to engage readers (the first of whom would be my skeptical professors) with history from a new angle; how to overcome the sense of implausibility that I had felt when the idea of American Indian contributions to the national revolutionary heritage was first presented to me.

Immersion in the records of the time had surprised me. I had not realized how tightly Franklin's experience with the Iroquois had been woven into his development of revolutionary theory and his advocacy of federal union. To understand how all this had come to be, I had to remove myself as much as possible from the assumptions of the twentieth century, to try to visualize America as Franklin knew it.

I would need to describe the Iroquois he knew, not celluloid caricatures concocted from bogus history, but well-organized polities governed by a system that one contemporary of Franklin's, Cadwallader Colden, wrote had "outdone the Romans." Colden was writing of a social and political system so old that the immigrant Europeans knew nothing of its origins—a federal union of five (and later six) Indian nations that had put into practice concepts of popular participation and natural rights that the European savants had thus far only theorized. The Iroquoian system, expressed through its constitution, "The Great Law of Peace," rested on assumptions foreign to the monarchies of Europe: it regarded leaders as servants of the people, rather than their masters, and made provisions for the leaders' impeachment for errant behavior. The Iroquois' law and custom upheld freedom of expression in political and religious matters, and it forbade the unauthorized entry of homes. It provided for political participation by women and the relatively equitable distribution of wealth. These distinctly democratic tendencies sound familiar in light of subsequent American political history—yet few people today (other than American Indians and students of their heritage) know that a republic existed on our soil before anyone here had ever heard of John Locke, or Cato, the *Magna Charta,* Rousseau, Franklin, or Jefferson.

To describe the Iroquoian system would not be enough, however. I would have to show how the unique geopolitical context of the mid–eighteenth century brought together Iroquois and Colonial leaders—the dean of whom was Franklin—in an atmosphere favoring the communication of political and social ideas: how, in

[*xiv*]

essence, the American frontier became a laboratory for democracy precisely at a time when Colonial leaders were searching for alternatives to what they regarded as European tyranny and class stratification.

Once assembled, the pieces of this historical puzzle assumed an amazingly fine fit. The Iroquois, the premier Indian military power in eastern North America, occupied a pivotal geographical position between the rival French of the St. Lawrence Valley and the English of the Eastern Seaboard. Barely a million Anglo-Americans lived in communities scattered along the East Coast, islands in a sea of American Indian peoples that stretched far inland, as far as anyone who spoke English then knew, into the boundless mountains and forests of a continent much larger than Europe. The days when Euro-Americans could not have survived in America without Indian help had passed, but the new Americans still were learning to wear Indian clothing, eat Indian corn and potatoes, and follow Indian trails and watercourses, using Indian snowshoes and canoes. Indians and Europeans were more often at peace than at war—a fact missed by telescoped history that focuses on conflict.

At times, Indian peace was as important to the history of the continent as Indian war, and the mid–eighteenth century was such a time. Out of English efforts at alliance with the Iroquois came a need for treaty councils, which brought together leaders of both cultures. And from the earliest days of his professional life, Franklin was drawn to the diplomatic and ideological interchange of these councils—first as a printer of their proceedings, then as a Colonial envoy, the beginning of one of the most distinguished diplomatic careers in American history. Out of these councils grew an early campaign by Franklin for Colonial union on a federal model, very similar to the Iroquois system.

Contact with Indians and their ways of ordering life left a definite imprint on Franklin and others who were seeking, during the prerevolutionary period, alternatives to a European order against which revolution would be made. To Jefferson, as well as Franklin, the Indians had what the colonists wanted: societies free of oppression and class stratification. The Iroquois and other Indian nations fired the imaginations of the revolution's architects. As Henry Steele Commager has written, America acted the Enlightenment as European radicals dreamed it. Extensive, intimate contact with Indian nations was a major reason for this difference.

This book has two major purposes. First, it seeks to weave a few new threads into the tapestry of American revolutionary history, to begin the telling of a larger story that has lain largely forgotten, scattered around dusty archives, for more than two centuries. By arguing that American Indians (principally the Iroquois) played a major role in shaping the ideas of Franklin (and thus, the American Revolution) I do not mean to demean or denigrate European influences. I mean not to subtract from the existing record, but to add an indigenous aspect, to show how America has been a creation of all its peoples.

In the telling, this story also seeks to demolish what remains of stereotypical assumptions that American Indians were somehow too simpleminded to engage in effective social and political organization. No one may doubt any longer that there has been more to history, much more, than the simple opposition of "savagery" and "civilization." History's popular writers have served us with many kinds of savages, noble and vicious, "good Indians" and "bad Indians," nearly always as beings too preoccupied with the essentials of the hunt to engage in philosophy and statecraft.

This was simply not the case. Franklin and his fellow founders knew differently. They learned from American Indians, by assimilating into their vision of the future, aspects of American Indian wisdom and beauty. Our task is to relearn history as they experienced it, in all its richness and complexity, and thereby to arrive at a more complete understanding of what we were, what we are, and what we may become.

—Bruce E. Johansen
Seattle, Washington
July 1981

FORGOTTEN

FOUNDERS

CHAPTER ONE

A Composite Culture

When the Roman legions conquered Greece, Roman historians
wrote with as little imagination as did the European historians
who have written of the white man's conquest of America. . . .
—Felix Cohen,
"Americanizing the White Man,"
American Scholar, 1952

After Christopher Columbus's first encounter with a continent
that he initially mistook for India, North America became the
permanent home of several markedly different cultural and ethnic
groups. The "Age of Discovery" that Columbus initiated in 1492
was also an age of cultural interchange between the peoples of Europe and the Americas. Each learned from the other, borrowing
artifacts—and ideas. This traffic continues today. The result of
such extensive communication across cultural lines has produced
in contemporary North America a composite culture that is rich
in diversity, and of a type unique in the world.

The creation of this culture began with first contact—possibly
long before Columbus's landing. Fragments of pottery that resemble Japanese patterns have been found in present-day Equa-
dor, dated well before the birth of Christ. The Vikings left some

[3]

tools behind in northeast North America. But while pottery, tools, and other things may be traced and dated, ideas are harder to follow through time. Thus, while the introduction of new flora, fauna, and tools has been given some study, the communication of ideas has been neglected.

American Indians visited Europe before the Pilgrims landed at Plymouth Rock. Squanto, a Wampanoag, one of several Indians kidnapped from their native land (the immigrants called it New England), visited England during 1614 and returned home in time to meet the somewhat bewildered Pilgrims, who arrived during the fall of 1620, unprepared for winter on a continent that, to them, was as new as it was forbidding. It was Squanto who surprised the Pilgrims by greeting them in English and who helped the new immigrants survive that first winter, a season that produced the first Thanksgiving. At that first feast, Indians provided the Europeans with turkey, one of the best-remembered examples of cultural interchange in United States popular history. For his role in acculturating these English subjects to a new land, Squanto has been called a Pilgrim father.

During the years following the landing of the Pilgrims, American Indians contributed many foods to the diet of a growing number of Euro-Americans. By the twentieth century, almost half the world's domesticated crops, including the staples—corn and white potatoes—were first cultivated by American Indians. Aside from turkey, corn, and white potatoes, Indians also contributed manoic, sweet potatoes, squash, peanuts, peppers, pumpkins, tomatoes, pineapples, the avocado, cacao (chocolate), chicle (a constituent of chewing gum), several varieties of beans, and at least seventy other domesticated food plants. Almost all the cotton grown in the United States was derived from varieties originally cultivated by Indians. Rubber, too, was contributed by native Americans.

Several American Indian medicines also came into use among

Euro-Americans. These included quinine, laxatives, as well as several dozen other drugs and herbal medicines. Euro-Americans adapted to their own needs many Indian articles of clothing and other artifacts such as hammocks, kayaks, canoes, moccasins, smoking pipes, dog sleds, and parkas. With the plants and artifacts came the Indian words used to describe them, and other features of what, to the Europeans, was a new land. Half the states in the United States of America today bear names first spoken among Indians; the thousands of words that entered English and other European languages from American Indian sources are too numerous even to list in this brief survey.

Assertions have also been made that Indian contributions helped shape Euro-American folksongs, locations for railroads and highways, ways of dying cloth, war tactics, and even bathing habits. The amount of communication from Indians to Euro-Americans was all the more surprising because Indians usually made no conscious effort to convert the colonists to their ways. While Euro-Americans often used trade and gift giving to introduce, and later sell, products of their cultures to Indians, Euro-American adoption of Indian artifacts, unlike some of those from Euro-Americans to Indians, was completely voluntary. In the words of Max Savelle, scholar of the revolutionary period, Indian artifacts "were to contribute their own ingredients to the amalgam that was to be America's civilization." This influence was woven into the lives of Europeans in America despite the fact that Indians lacked organized means of propagation, but simply because they were useful and necessary to life in the New World.

Unlike the physical aspects of this amalgam, the intellectual contributions of American Indians to Euro-American culture have only lightly, and for the most part recently, been studied by a few historians, anthropologists, scholars of law, and others. Where physical artifacts may be traced more or less directly, the communication of ideas may, most often, only be inferred from those islands of knowledge remaining in written records. These written records are almost exclusively of Euro-American origin, and often leave blind spots that may be partly filled only by records based on Indian oral history.

Paul Bohanan, writing in the introduction of *Beyond the Frontier* (1967), which he coedited with Fred Plog, stressed the need to "tear away the veils of ethnocentricism," which he asserted have often kept scholars from seeing that peoples whom they had relegated to the category of "primitive" possessed "institutions as complex and histories as full as our own." A. Irving Hallowell, to make a similar point, quoted Bernard de Voto:

> *Most American history has been written as if history were a function soley of white culture—in spite of the fact that well into the nineteenth century the Indians were one of the principal determinants of historical events. Those of us who work in frontier history are repeatedly nonplussed to discover how little has been done for us in regard to the one force bearing on our field that was active everywhere. . . . American historians have made shockingly little effort to understand the life, the societies, the cultures, the thinking and the feeling of the Indians, and disastrously little effort to understand how all these affected white men and their societies.* *

To De Voto's assertion, Hallowell added: "Since most history has been written by the conquerers, the influence of the primitive people upon American civilization has seldom been the subject of dispassionate consideration."

---

* A. Irving Hallowell, "The Backwash of the Frontier: The Impact of the Indian on American Culture," in Walker D. Wyman and Clifton B. Kroeber, eds., *The Frontier in Perspective* (Madison: University of Wisconsin Press, 1957), p. 230.

A Composite Culture

Felix Cohen, author of the *Handbook of Indian Law*, the basic reference book of his field, also advised a similar course of study and a similar break with prevailing ethnocentricism. Writing in the *American Scholar* (1952), Cohen said:

> When the Roman legions conquered Greece, Roman historians wrote with as little imagination as did the European historians who have written of the white man's conquest of America. What the Roman historians did not see was that captive Greece would take captive conquering Rome and that Greek science, Greek philosphy and a Greek book, known as Septaugint, *translated into the Latin tongue, would guide the civilized world and bring the tramp of pilgrim feet to Rome a thousand years after the last Roman regiment was destroyed.*

American historians, wrote Cohen, had too often paid attention to military victories and changing land boundaries, while failing to "see that in agriculture, in government, in sport, in education and in our views of nature and our fellow men, it is the first Americans who have taken captive their battlefield conquerers." American historians "have seen America only as an imitation of Europe," Cohen asserted. In his view, "The real epic of America is the yet unfinished story of the Americanization of the white man."

Cohen's broad indictment does not include all scholars, nor all historians. The question of American Indian influence on the intellectual traditions of Euro-American culture has been raised, especially during the last thirty years. These questions, however, have not yet been examined in the depth that the complexity of Indian contributions warrant.

To raise such questions is not to ignore, nor to negate, the profound influence of Europe on American intellectual development.

[7   ]

It is, rather, to add a few new brush strokes to an as yet unfinished portrait. It is to explore the intellectual trade between cultures that has made America unique, built from contributions not only by Europeans and American Indians, but also by almost every other major cultural and ethnic group that has taken up residence in the Americas.

What follows is only a first step, tracing the way in which Benjamin Franklin and some of his contemporaries, including Thomas Jefferson, absorbed American Indian political and social ideas, and how some of these ideas were combined with the cultural heritage they had brought from Europe into a rationale for revolution in a new land. There is a case to be made in that American Indian thought helped make that possible.*

Comparison of the Iroquois' system of government with that of the new United States' began with Lewis Henry Morgan, known as the "father of American anthropology," who produced in 1851 the first systematic study of an American Indian social organization in his *League of the Ho-de-no-sau-nee, or Iroquois*. Following more than a decade of close association with the Iroquois, especially Ely Parker (the Seneca who helped arrange Morgan's adoption by the Iroquois), Morgan observed:

> *Among the Indian nations whose ancient seats were within the limits of our republic, the Iroquois have long continued to occupy the most conspicuous position. They achieved for themselves a more remarkable civil organization and acquired a higher degree of influence than any race of Indian lineage, except those of Mexico and Peru.*

Morgan likened the federalism of the Iroquois to that of the newly united British colonies: "The [six] nations sustained nearly the

---

* Henry Steele Commager discusses this theme in *The Empire of Reason: How Europe Imagined and America Realized the Enlightenment* (Garden City, NY: Doubleday, 1977).

same relation to the [Iroquois] league that the American states bear to the Union. In the former, several oligarchies were contained within one, in the same manner as in the latter, several republics are embraced in one republic." Morgan also noted checks and balances in the Iroquoian system that acted to prevent concentration of power: "Their whole civil policy was averse to the concentration of power in the hands of any single individual, but inclined to the opposite principle of division among a number of equals." The Iroquois, according to Morgan, maximized individual freedom while seeking to minimize excess governmental interference in peoples' lives: "The government sat lightly upon the people who, in effect, were governed but little. It secured to each that individual independence which the Ho-de-no-sau-nee knew how to prize as well as the Saxon race; and which, amid all their political changes, they have continued to preserve."

"The People of the Longhouse commended to our forefathers a union of colonies similar to their own as early as 1755," Morgan wrote. "They [the Iroquois] saw in the common interests and common speech of the colonies the elements for a confederation." Morgan believed that the Iroquois Confederacy contained "the germ of modern parliament, congress, and legislature."

Morgan's major works have been widely reprinted in the United States and in several other countries during the century and a half since he first sat around the Iroquois Confederacy's council fire with his newly acquired brothers. In some of these editions, the idea of Iroquois influence on the formation of the United States' political and social system have been raised anew. Herbert M. Lloyd, in an introduction to the 1902 Dodd, Mead and Company edition of *League of the Iroquois*, wrote:

Among all the North American peoples, there is none more worthy of study, by reason of their intellectual ability, the character of their institutions and the part they have played

in history, than the Iroquois of the League. And, as it hap-
pens, this is the people which has longest been known to
ourselves, which has been most closely observed by our writ-
ers and statesmen, and whose influence has been most
strongly felt in our political constitution and in our history
as colonies and nation.

Lloyd continued: "In their ancient League the Iroquois presented to us a type of Federal Republic under whose roof and around whose council fire all people might dwell in peace and freedom. Our nation gathers its people from many peoples of the Old World, its language and its free institutions it inherits from England, its civilization and art from Greece and Rome, its religion from Judea—and even these red men of the forest have wrought some of the chief stones in our national temple."

In an early history of the relations between Sir William Johnson and the Iroquois, William E. Griffis in 1891 advised further study of Iroquoian influence on the formation of the United States, especially Benjamin Franklin's role in this interaction. At the beginning of the twentieth century Arthur C. Parker, son of the Ely Parker who had been close to Morgan, wrote in a preface to his version of the Iroquois Great Law of Peace:

Here, then, we find the right of popular nomination, the
right of recall and of woman suffrage flourishing in the old
America of the Red Man and centuries before it became the
clamor of the new America of the white invader. Who now
shall call the Indians and Iroquois savages?

A similar point of view was taken in 1918 by J. N. B. Hewitt, who not only suggested that the Iroquois influenced the formation of the United States, but that the Iroquois league also served as something of a prototype for the League of Nations.

The Iroquois' Great Law of Peace, wrote Hewitt, "made a significant departure from the past in separating the conduct of military and civilian affairs." The confederacy, he continued, also recognized no state religion: "All forms of it [religion] were tolerated and practiced." The Iroquois polity separated the duties of civil chiefs and prophets, or other religious leaders. Hewitt also noted the elevated position of women in the Iroquois system of government.

In 1930, Arthur Pound's *Johnson of the Mohawks* again introduced the possibility of intellectual communication: "With the possible exception of the also unwritten British Constitution deriving from the *Magna Charta*, the Iroquois Constitution is the longest-going international constitution in the world." Pound remarked at the "political sagacity" of the Iroquois, as well as the checks and balances built into the Iroquois league, which was structured in such a way that no action could be taken without the approval of all five represented Indian nations. It was Pound's belief that "in this constitution of the Five Nations are found practically all of the safeguards which have been raised in historic parliaments to protect home affairs from centralized authority."

Carl Van Doren's biography of Benjamin Franklin, published in 1938, noted Franklin's admiration of the political system of the league, and suggested that his plans for a Colonial union, expressed first during the 1750s, owed some debt to the Iroquois. Franklin, Van Doren wrote, found no European model that was suitable for the needs of the colonies that he hoped to unite.

In 1940 Clark Wissler asserted that "students of politics and government have found much to admire in the league [of the Iroquois]. There is some historical evidence that knowledge of the league influenced the colonists in their first attempts to form a confederacy and later to write a constitution."* Five years later, Frank G. Speck, finding the Iroquois "a decidedly democratic

---

* Clark Wissler, *Indians of the United States: Four Centuries of Their History and Culture* (Garden City, NY: Doubleday, 1940), pp. 112–113.

[11   ]

people,"* quoted Wissler to support his contention that the Iroquois played a role in the founding of the United States. Wissler mentioned advice, given by the Iroquois chief Canassatego at the Lancaster (Pennsylvania) treaty of 1744, to the effect that the colonists could benefit by forming a union along Iroquoian lines.

By 1946, the nations of the world had established a second international organization and, as in 1918, attention was turned to the Iroquois in this regard. Paul A. W. Wallace, who devoted his scholarship to a study of the Iroquois, used quotations from the Great Law of Peace and the Preamble to the Constitution of the United Nations to open and close his book, the *White Roots of Peace*:

> I am Deganwidah, and with the Five Nations confederate lords I plant the tree of the Great Peace. . . . Roots have spread out from the Tree . . . and the name of these Roots is the Great White Roots of Peace. If any man or any nation outside the Five Nations shall show a desire to obey the laws of the Great Peace . . . they may trace the Roots to their source . . . and they shall be welcomed to take shelter beneath the Tree. . . .

> We, the peoples of the United Nations, determined to save succeeding generations from the scourge of war . . . and to reaffirm faith in fundamental human rights . . . and to establish conditions under which justice and respect for law can be maintained . . . do hereby establish an international organization to be known as the United Nations.

While Wallace's *White Roots of Peace* was principally an account of the traditional story of the creation of the Iroquois league, he also mentioned Franklin's attention to Iroquois politi-

---

* See: Frank G. Speck, "The Iroquois, A Study in Cultural Evolution" (Bloomfield Hills, Michigan: Cranbrook Institute of Science, *Bulletin* 23, October 1945).

cal institutions and the possible role that this attention played in the founding of the United States.

By 1952, suggestions of Iroquoian contributions to the evolution of the United States' political structure, as well as that of international bodies, had been "in the air" of Euro-American scholarship for more than a century. During that year, Felix Cohen began to develop the idea in the *American Scholar*. Cohen wrote that in their rush to "Americanize" the Indian, Euro-Americans had forgotten, or chosen to ignore, that they had themselves been influenced by Indian thought and action. To Cohen, American disrespect for established authority had Indian roots, as did the American penchant for sharing with those in need. In the Indian character resided a fierce individuality that rejected subjugation, together with a communalism that put the welfare of the whole family, tribe, or nation above that of individuals.

"It is out of a rich Indian democratic tradition that the distinctive political ideals of American life emerged," Cohen wrote. "Universal suffrage for women as well as for men, the pattern of states within a state we call federalism, the habit of treating chiefs as servants of the people instead of as their masters . . ." Cohen ascribed at least in part to the "Indian" in our political tradition. To this, Cohen added: "The insistence that the community must respect the diversity of men and the diversity of their dreams—all these things were part of the American way of life before Columbus landed." To support his assertion, Cohen offered an excerpt from a popular account of America that was circulated in England around 1776: "The darling passion of the American is liberty and that in its fullest extent; nor is it the original natives only to whom this passion is confined; our colonists sent thither seem to have imbibed the same principles."*

---

* Felix Cohen, "Americanizing the White Man," *American Scholar* 21: 2 (1952), p. 181.

"Politically, there was nothing in the Empires and kingdoms of Europe in the fifteenth and sixteenth centuries to parallel the democratic constitution of the Iroquois Confederacy, with its provisions for initiative, referendum and recall, and its suffrage for women as well as for men," Cohen continued. The influence of such ideas spread to Europe, where they played a part in Thomas More's *Utopia*. Cohen further asserted that "to John Locke, the champion of tolerance and the right of revolution, the state of nature and of natural equality to which men might appeal in rebellion against tyranny was set not in the remote dawn of history, but beyond the Atlantic sunset." Cohen also found the influence of Indian thought in Montesquieu, Voltaire, and Rousseau, "and their various contemporaries." Anticipating the arguments of Charles Sanford nine years later, Cohen implied that many of the doctrines that played so crucial a role in the American Revolution were fashioned by European savants from observation of the New World and its inhabitants. These observations, packaged into theories, were exported, like the finished products made from raw materials that also traveled the Atlantic Ocean, back to America. The communication among American Indian cultures, Europe, and Euro-America thus seemed to involve a sort of intellectual mercantilism. The product of this intellectual traffic, the theories that played a role in rationalizing rebellion against England, may have been fabricated in Europe, but the raw materials from which they were made were, to Cohen, substantially of indigenous American origin.

Cohen, continuing his synthesis of a hundred years of suggestions that Indian ideas helped shape America's and Europe's intellectual traditions, asserted that "the greatest teachers of American democracy have gone to school with the Indian." He mentioned Canassatego's advice to the colonists at the 1744 Lancaster treaty, and asserted that Benjamin Franklin had integrated this advice into his ideas favoring Colonial union seven years later.

Cohen also asserted that Thomas Jefferson freely acknowledged his debt to the conceptions of liberty held by American Indians, and favorably compared the liberty he saw in Indian politics with the oppression of Europe in his time.

Following publication of Cohen's article, suggestions that American Indian, and especially Iroquoian, thought had played some role in the genesis of a distinctly American conception of society and government became more numerous. In 1953, Ruth Underhill (*Red Man's Continent*) wrote that Franklin, Jefferson, John Adams, and George Washington all were familiar with the Iroquois polity, which, she said, "was the most integrated and orderly north of Mexico. Some have even thought that it gave suggestions to the American Constitution." Underhill also devoted some attention to the equality of women, and the political powers reserved for them, in the Iroquois structure. Like Wallace before her, Underhill also asserted similarity between the Iroquoian system and the modern United Nations. Both, she wrote, "dealt only with international concerns of peace and war."

In 1955, Thomas R. Henry, in an account of the history of the Iroquois Confederacy, picked up Hewitt's suggestion of intercultural communication. Hewitt, wrote Henry, had used Canassatego's 1744 speech and a remembrance of it in a 1775 treaty council to support his assertion that the Six Nations had played a role in the formation of the United States. "J. N. B. Hewitt was firmly convinced that the League of the Iroquois was the intellectual progenitor of the United States." While acknowledging Hewitt's argument, Henry wrote that more research in the area needed to be done.

A. Irving Hallowell in 1957 mentioned the subject of intellectual origins of the American republic in connection with the Iroquois, but did not delve into it. "It has been said that information about the organization and operation of the League of the Iroquois which Franklin picked up at various Indian councils suggested to him the pattern for a United States of America." He also advised more study of these suggestions.

In 1960, author Edmund Wilson, having traveled to Iroquois country to research his book, *Apologies to the Iroquois,* heard an oral-history account from Standing Arrow, a Seneca, of the reliance that Franklin had placed on the Great Law of Peace. He did not pursue the subject in the book.

In 1961, Charles Sanford's *Quest for Paradise* again raised the possibility of intellectual mercantilism. Like Frederick Jackson Turner, originator of the "Frontier Hypothesis" who found democracy inexplicibly emerging from among the trees, Sanford stressed the effect of the New World's geography over its inhabitants, but he still found a few Indians in the forest that he characterized as a new Eden:

> The archetypical Adam, living in a state of nature was thus endowed by his creators, which included Thomas Jefferson, with inalienable rights to life, liberty and the pursuit of happiness. The revolutionary doctrines which grew out of discoveries of the New World were first developed by European savants only to be borrowed by the American colonists and turned against Europe.

In 1965, William Brandon wrote that more attention should be paid to "the effect of the Indian world on the changing American soul, most easily seen in the influence of the American Indian on European notions of liberty." Brandon asserted that the first British inter-Colonial union of any kind, the New England Confederation of 1643, came about "not only as a result of the Pequot War but possibly in some imitation of the many Indian confederacies . . . in aboriginal North America." The first formal inter-Colonial conference outside of New England, which took place in Albany in 1684, "was held at the urging of the Iroquois and to meet with

Iroquois spokesmen," Brandon wrote.* He also described accounts by Peter Martyr, the first historian of the New World, which enthusiastically told of the Indians' liberty, the absence of crime and jails, and the greed that accompanied a societal emphasis on private property. Martyr and other Europeans of his time wondered whether, in Brandon's words, the Indians lived "in that golden world of which the ancients had spoken so much." Out of such imagery came the myth of the Noble Savage, another product of the intellectual mercantilism that seemed to accompany its economic counterpart across the Atlantic Ocean. Out of such imagery, too, came the assumption that Indians, at least those Indians still uncorrupted by European influences, lived in the original state of all societies and that, by observing them, the new arrivals from Europe could peer through a living window on their own pasts. To many who had recently escaped poverty, or fled tyranny in Europe, this was a vision of the past that must have carried no small amount of appeal.

During 1967, C. Elmore Reaman's work on the Iroquois' role in the conflict between the British and French during the mid-eighteenth century again raised the possibility of Iroquoian influence on the founding of the United States: "Any race of people who provided the prototype for the Constitution of the United States, and whose confederacy has many of the aspects of the present-day United Nations, should be given their rightful recognition." Reaman supported his assertion by quoting from a speech given by Richard Pilant on Iroquoian studies at McMaster University April 6, 1960: "Unlike the Mayas and Incas to the south, the Longhouse People developed a democratic system of government which can be maintained [to be] a prototype for the United States and the United Nations. Socially, the Six Nations

* William Brandon, "American Indians and American History," *American West* 13 (1965), p. 24.

met the sociologist's test of higher cultures by having given a preferred status to women." Reaman added that the Iroquois league, in his estimation, "was a model social order in many ways superior to the white man's culture of the day. . . . Its democratic form of government more nearly approached perfection than any that has been tried to date. It is claimed by many that the framers of the United States of America copied from these Iroquois practices in founding the government of the United States." This material was based on Hewitt's work.

Throughout the next few years, a thread of interest in the Iroquois' communication of political ideas to the new United States continued to run through literature in this area of history. In 1968, Allan W. Eckert wrote:

> *The whites who were versed in politics at this time [c. 1750] had every reason to marvel at this form of Indian government. Knowledge of the league's success, it is believed, strongly influenced the colonies in their own initial efforts to form a union and later to write a Constitution.*

In 1971, Helen A. Howard borrowed part of Wallace's *White Roots of Peace*, including the paired quotations from the Great Law of Peace and the United Nations' Constitution, to raise the question of Iroquoian intellectual influence. During the same year, Mary E. Mathur's Ph. D. dissertation at the University of Wisconsin asserted that the plan of union that Franklin proposed at the Albany congress (1754) more closely resembled the Iroquoian model than the British. Mathur placed major emphasis on an appearance by Hendrick, an Iroquois statesman, at the congress. She also asserted, but did not document, reports that Felix Cohen had read accounts written by British spies shortly before the Revolutionary War that blamed the Iroquois and other Indians' notions of liberty for the colonists' resistance to British rule.

A European, Elemire Zolla, in 1973 recounted Horatio Hale's

belief, published in *The Iroquois Book of Rites,* that democracy sprang mainly from Indian origins. Zolla also recounted Edmund Wilson's encounter with Standing Arrow and the Senecas. In 1975, J. E. Chamberlin's *The Harrowing of Eden* noted that "it is generally held that the model of the great Iroquois [Six Nations] Confederacy was a significant influence on both the Albany plan and the later Articles of Confederation." In a footnote to that reference, Chamberlin wrote that the Iroquois had also exerted influence on Karl Marx and Frederich Engels through Lewis H. Morgan. Engels, having read Morgan's *Ancient Society* (1877), wrote *The Origin of the Family, Private Property and the State, in Light of the Researchers of Lewis Henry Morgan* (1884), which contained an intricate account of the Iroquoian polity that most directly examined the league's ability to maintain social cohesion without an elaborate state apparatus. The Iroquois, wrote Engels, provided a rare example of a living society that "knows no state."*

Francis Jennings's finely detailed work, *The Invasion of America: Indians, Colonialism and the Cant of Conquest* (1975), closed a discussion that noted Euro-Americans' perceptions of Indians' liberty with a sweeping statement: "What white society owes to Indian society, as much as to any other source, is the mere fact of its existence."

Donald A. Grinde in 1979 collected much of what had been written about the subject of Iroquoian intellectual interaction with English-speaking Euro-Americans. While his *The Iroquois and the Founding of the American Nation* was mostly a military and diplomatic account of the Iroquois' role during the time period around the American Revolution, it also contained most of the published evidence in secondary sources on this topic. Grinde reserved special attention for the interaction of Franklin and Jef-

---

* Frederich Engels, *The Origin of the Family, Private Property and the State,* in Marx and Engels, *Selected Works* (New York: International Publishers, 1968), p. 527.

ferson with the Iroquois, and urged more study of the matter: "More needs to be done. Especially if America continues to view itself as a distinct entity set apart from many of the values of Western Civilization." Grinde also stated that such study could help dissolve negative stereotypes that many Euro-Americans harbor about American Indians' heritage.

The negation of stereotypes is important to this investigation because to study the intellectual contributions of American Indians to European and American thought, one must to some degree abolish the polarity of the "civilized" and the "savage" that much of our history (not to mention popular entertainment) has drilled into us. We must approach the subject ready to be surprised, as our ancestors were surprised when they were new to America. We must be ready to acknowledge that American Indian societies were as thoughtfully constructed and historically significant to our present as the Romans, the Greeks, and other Old World peoples.

What follows is only a beginning. The Iroquois were not the only American Indians to develop notions of federalism, political liberty, and democracy long before they heard of the Greeks or the *Magna Charta*. Benjamin Franklin was not the only Euro-American to combine his own heritage with what he found in his new homeland. And the infant United States was not the only nation whose course has been profoundly influenced by the ideas of the Indians, the forgotten cofounders of our heritage.

CHAPTER TWO

The Pre-Columbian Republic

The chiefs of the League of Five Nations shall be mentors of the
people for all time. The thickness of their skins shall be seven
spans . . . their minds filled with a yearning for the welfare of the
people of the League. . . .
> —The Great Law of Peace, Paragraph 24,
> Akwesasne Notes version, 1977
> Mohawk Nation, New York

When the Iroquois Confederacy was formed, no Europeans were
present with clocks and a system for telling time before and after
the birth of Christ. Since ideas, unlike artifacts, cannot be carbon
dated or otherwise fixed in unrecorded time, the exact date that
the Senecas, Onondagas, Oneidas, Mohawks, and Cayugas
stopped battling one another and formed a federal union will
never be known. It is known, however, that around 1714 the Tuscaroras, a kindred Indian nation, moved northward from what is
presently the Carolinas to become the sixth national member of
the confederacy.

A wide range of estimates exist for the founding date of the
confederacy. Iroquoian sources, using oral history and recollec-
tions of family ancestries (the traditional methods for marking

time through history), have fixed the origin date at between 1000 and 1400 A.D.; Euro-American historians have tended to place the origin of the Iroquois league at about 1450.

By an Iroquois account, Cartier made his first appearance among the Iroquois during the life of the thirty-third presiding chief of the league. The presiding chief (*Atotarho* was the name of the office) held a lifetime appointment unless he was impeached for violating the Great Law of Peace. The Iroquois who use this method of tracing the league's origin place the date at between 1000 and 1100. Arthur C. Parker, a Seneca, used Iroquoian recall of family lines and lifespans to estimate the founding date at 1390. Paul A. W. Wallace, a student of the Iroquois who has written extensively about them, estimated the founding date of the league at 1450. This is only a sample of the attempts that have been made to solve an unsolvable riddle.

At whatever date the confederacy was formed, it came at the end of several generations of bloody and divisive warfare between the five nations that joined the league. According to the Iroquois' traditional account, the idea of a federal union was introduced through Deganwidah, a Huron who lived in what is now eastern Ontario. Deganwidah was unsuited himself to propose the idea not only because of his non-Iroquoian ancestry, but also because he stuttered so badly that he could scarcely talk. He would have had the utmost difficulty in presenting his idea to societies where oratory was prized. And writing, aside from the pictographs of the wampum belts, was not used.

Deganwidah, wandering from tribe to tribe trying to figure ways to realize his dream of ending war among them all, met Hiawatha, who agreed to speak for him. Hiawatha (a man far removed from Longfellow's poetic creation) undertook long negotiations with leaders of the warring Indian nations and, in the end, produced a peace along the lines of Deganwidah's vision.

This peace was procured, and maintained, through the constitution of the league, the Great Law of Peace (untranslated: *Kaianerekowa*). The story of the Great Law's creation is no less rich in history and allegory than the stories of cultural origin handed down by European peoples, and is only briefly summarized here.

The Great Law of Peace was not written in English until about 1880 when Seth Newhouse, a Mohawk, transcribed it. By this time, many of the traditional sachems of the league, worried that the wampum belts that contained the Great Law's provisions might be lost or stolen, sought a version written in English. One such translation was compiled by Arthur C. Parker. In recent years, the text of the Great Law has been published in several editions by *Akwesasne Notes*, a journal for "native and natural peoples" published on the Mohawk Nation. The substance of all these written translations is similar, although wording varies at some points.

The text of the Great Law begins with the planting of the Tree of the Great Peace; the great white pine—from its roots to its spreading branches—serves throughout the document as a metaphor for the unity of the league. The tree, and the principal council fire of the confederacy, were located on land of the Onondaga Nation, at the center of the confederacy, the present site of Syracuse, New York.

From the Tree of the Great Peace

Roots have spread out . . . one to the north, one to the west, one to the east and one to the south. These are the Great White Roots and their nature is peace and strength. If any man or any nation outside the Five Nations shall obey the laws of the Great Peace and shall make this known to the statesmen of the League, they may trace back the roots to the tree. If their minds are clean and they are obedient and promise to obey the wishes of the Council of the League, they shall be welcomed to take shelter beneath the Tree of the Long Leaves.

This opening provision complements the adoption laws of the confederacy, which contained no bars on the basis of race or national origin. Nor did the Great Law prohibit dual citizenship; several influential Anglo-Americans, emissaries from the Colonial governments, including William Johnson and Conrad Weiser, were given full citizenship in the confederacy. Both men took part in the deliberations of the Grand Council at Onondaga.

Following paragraphs three and four, which outlined procedural matters such as the calling of meetings and maintenance of the council fire, the Great Law began to outline a complex system of checks and balances on the power of each nation against that of the others. The Great Law ensured that no measure (such as a declaration of war) would be enacted by the Council of the League without the consent of all five represented nations, each of which would first debate the question internally:

> The council of the Mohawks shall be divided into three parties . . . the first party shall listen only to the discussion of the second and third parties and if an error is made, or the proceeding irregular, they are to call attention to it, and when the case is right and properly decided by the two parties, they shall confirm the decision and refer the case to the Seneca statesmen for their decision. When the Seneca statesmen have decided in accord with the Mohawk statesmen, the case or question shall be referred to the Cayuga and Oneida statesmen on the opposite side of the house.

After a question had been debated by the Mohawks, Senecas, Oneidas, and Cayugas on both sides of the "house," it was passed to the Onondagas, the firekeepers, for their decision. The Great Law provided that every Onondaga statesman or his deputy be present in council and that all agree with the majority "without unwarrantable dissent." Decisions, when made, had to be unanimous. If *Atotarho*, or other chiefs among the Onondaga delegation were absent, the council could only decide on matters of small importance.

If the decision of the "older brothers" (Senecas and Mohawks) disagreed with that of the "younger brothers" (Cayugas and Oneidas), the Onondagas were charged with breaking the tie. If the four nations agreed, the Onondagas were instructed by the Great Law to confirm the decision. The Onondagas could, however, refuse to confirm a decision given them by the other four nations, and send it back for reconsideration. If the four nations rendered the same decision again, the Onondagas had no other course but to confirm it. This decision-making process somewhat resembled that of a two-house congress in one body, with the "older brothers" and "younger brothers" each comprising a side of the house. The Onondagas filled something of an executive role, with a veto that could be overriden by the older and younger brothers in concert.*

Paragraph 14 of the Great Law provided that the speaker for any particular meeting of the council would be elected by acclamation from either the Mohawks, Senecas, or Onondagas. The Great Law also provided for changes to the Great Law, by way of amendment:

> If the conditions which arise at any future time call for an addition to or a change of this law, the case shall be carefully considered and if a new beam seems necessary or beneficial, the proposed change shall be decided upon and, if adopted, shall be called "added to the rafters."

---

* The Tuscaroras had no voting rights after they joined the confederacy during the early eighteenth century.

The next major section of the Great Law concerned the rights, duties, and qualifications of statesmen. The chiefs who sat on the council were elected in two ways. Traditionally, they were nominated by the women of each extended family holding title (in the form of special wampum strings) to a chiefship. Increasingly during the seventeenth and eighteenth centuries, chiefs were elected outside this hereditary structure on the basis of their leadership qualities.

In order to keep his office, a chief had to abide by several rules, most of which were written into the Great Law. A chief could not, for example, refuse to attend meetings of the council. After one warning by the women who had nominated him, a chief who continued to ignore council meetings was removed.

More seriously, a chief could be removed from the council if it became "apparent . . . [that he] . . . has not in mind the welfare of the people, or [if he] disobeys the rules of the Great Law. . . ." Complaints about the conduct of chiefs could be brought before the council by "the men and women of the league, or both acting jointly," and communicated to the accused through the war chiefs who, in peacetime, often acted as the peoples' monitors on the other chiefs in council. An erring chief, after three warnings, would be removed by the war chiefs if complaints continued and the erring chief did not mend his ways.

One of the most serious offenses of which a chief could be accused was murder. The sanctions against this crime may have been made as stringent as they were because blood feuds were a major problem before Deganwidah united the Iroquois.

If a chief of the League of Five Nations should commit murder, the other chiefs of the nation shall assemble at the place where the corpse lies and prepare to depose the criminal chief. If it is impossible to meet at the scene of the crime the chiefs shall discuss the matter at the next council of their nation and request their war chief to depose the chief guilty of the crime, to "bury" his women relatives and to transfer the chieftanship title to a sister family.

The reference to burial was figurative; the law provided that a chief guilty of murder would not only lose his own title, but deprive his entire extended family of the right to be represented on the council. In addition, a chief guilty of murder was banished from the confederacy.

Certain physical and mental defects, such as idiocy, blindness, deafness, dumbness, or impotency could also cause a chief's dismissal from office, although the Great Law provided that "in cases of extreme necessity," the chief could continue to exercise his rights in council.

While holding membership on the confederate council, the Great Law provided that a chief should be tolerant and attentive to constituent criticism:

The chiefs of the League of Five Nations shall be mentors of the people for all time. The thickness of their skins shall be seven spans, which is to say that they shall be proof against anger, offensive action and criticism. Their hearts shall be full of peace and good will and their minds filled with a yearning for the welfare of the people of the League. With endless patience, they shall carry out their duty. Their firmness shall be tempered with a tenderness for their people. Neither anger nor fury shall find lodging in their minds and all their words and actions shall be marked by calm deliberation.

Paragraph 35 of the Great Law outlined provisions for election of "pine-tree chiefs"—those who held membership in the council because of their special abilities, rather than the hereditary titles of their extended families. The name "pine-tree chief" was given to such individuals because they were said to have sprung, like the

Great White Pine under which the council met. While the pine sprang from the earth, the pine-tree chiefs sprang from the body of the people. The nomination to the council came directly from the chiefs sitting on it.

A pine-tree chief could not be officially deposed, as could the hereditary chiefs, for violating the Great Law. If such a chief lost the confidence of the people, however, the Great Law told them to "be deaf to his voice and his advice." Like other civil chiefs, the pine-tree chiefs could not name their successors; nor could they carry their titles to the grave. The Great Law provided a ceremony for removing the title from a dying chief.

One war chief from each of the five represented nations also sat on the confederate council along with the hereditary and pine-tree chiefs. These chiefs were elected from the eligible sons of the female families holding title to the head chieftanship in each of the five nations. The war chiefs in peacetime acted as the peoples' eyes and ears in the council, carrying messages to and from the council and constituents. In wartime, these chiefs raised fighting forces, a task that often took no small amount of eloquence, since there was no enforced draft, and warriors had to be convinced that a cause was worth fighting for. It was also the duty of the war chief to lay questions of the people (other societies might call them petitions) before the Council of the League. War chiefs, like civil chiefs, could be recalled from office if they violated the Great Law's standards of leadership.

To prevent factions within the confederacy, Deganwidah and his confederates built into it a system of clans that overlapped each nations' political boundaries. The clans bore such names as Great Bear, Turtle, Deer Pigeon, Hawk, and Wild Potatoes. Each member of a particular clan recognized as a relative others of the same clan, even if they lived in different nations of the league. The clan structure and the system of checks and balances kept one nation from seeking to dominate others and helped to insure that consensus would arise from decisions of the council. Checks and balances were evident between the sexes, as well. Although the members of the Grand Council were men, most of them had been nominated by the women of their respective extended families. Women also were considered to be the allocators of resources, and descent was matrilineal.

Surely the first reference to a "United Nations" in American history occurred in paragraph 61 of the Great Law. A concept of national self-determination is expressed in paragraph 84, which allowed conquered non-Iroquoian nations, or those which peacefully accepted the Great Law, to continue their own system of internal government as long as it refrained from making war on other nations. Paragraph 98 confirmed the people's right to seek redress from the Grand Council through their respective war chiefs. Paragraph 99 guaranteed freedom of religion. Paragraph 107 denied entry to the home by those not authorized to do so by its occupants.

The Great Law was not wholly unwritten before its transcription into English during the late nineteenth century. Its provisions were recorded on wampum belts that were used during council meetings whenever disputes arose over procedure, or over the provisions of the law itself. Wampum was also used to record many other important events, such as contracts and other agreements. A contemporary source credits the belts with use "to assist the memory."*

---

* New York State Library Ms. #13350–51, reprinted in Charles M. Johnston, ed., *The Valley of the Six Nations: A Collection of Documents on Indian Lands of the Great River* (Toronto: The University of Toronto Press, 1964), pp. 28–29. Note that the wampum belts, used in this fashion, served as a set of symbols used to retain and convey meaning. Like the Aztecs (who kept tax records and other written materials), the Iroquois were not illiterate. Written communication evolved to fit specialized needs, and its utilization was restricted to a minority, not unlike the use of writing in Europe before the invention of the printing press.

"When a subject is of very great importance the belt is very wide and so on—if a Mohawk makes a promise to another, he gives him one of these belts—his word is irrevocable & they do not consider anything a greater reproach [than a] . . . word not binding," the same source recorded. Contrary to popular assumption many Indian cultures, the Iroquois among them, used some forms of written communication. These forms were only rarely appreciated by eighteenth-century Euro-American observers.

In addition to its use as an archive (usually kept by senior sachems), wampum also served as a medium of exchange. It had a definite value among the Iroquois and other Indians in relation to deerskins, beaver pelts, and (after extensive contact with Euro-Americans) British coins. Fashioned from conch and clam shells in the shape of beads, wampum was sewn into intricate patterns on hides. Each design had a different meaning, and understanding of the designs' meaning was indispensible to the conduct of Iroquoian diplomacy, as it was the *lingua franca* for conduct between nations (Indian to Indian and Indian to European) in North America for more than a century.

To do diplomatic business with the Iroquois, the British and French envoys had to learn how wampum was used. When the occasion called for giving, they should expect to get a string (often called a "strand" in treaty accounts) or a belt of wampum. A strand—beads strung on yard-long leather strips tied at one end—signified agreement on items of small importance, but still worth noting. Belts, often six feet long and up to two feet wide, were reserved for important items. The Iroquois dealt with the English and French only under their own diplomatic code, a way of reminding the Europeans that they were guests on the Indians' continent, which they called "Turtle Island." Euro-American diplomats who came to council without a sufficient supply of wampum strands and belts to give, or one who failed to understand the message of one or more belts, could make or break alliances at a time when the Iroquois' powerful confederacy and its Indian allies constituted the balance of power between the English and French in North America.

On a continent still very lightly settled with Europeans—islands of settlement in a sea of Indian nations—it behooved diplomatic suitors to know the difference between a peace and a war belt. It also helped to have Indian allies as guides through what Europeans regarded as a limitless and trackless wilderness. Without Indian help (on both sides) the Colonial wars in North America might have taken a great deal longer than they did. Without Indian guides, the armies would have had a much harder time finding one another, except by accident.

During the 1730s and 1740s, the British Crown decided that if it was to stem the French advance down the western side of the Appalachians, alliance with the Iroquois was imperative. The French advance south from the Saint Lawrence Valley and north from Louisiana threatened to hem the English between the mountains and the Atlantic. And so the peace belt went out in a diplomatic offensive that would end in France's defeat two decades later.

To win the Iroquois, the British envoys had to deal with the Iroquois on their own terms, as distasteful as this may have been to some of the more effete diplomats. They would find themselves sitting cross-legged around council fires many miles from the coastal cities, which Indian sachems refused to visit except on the most compelling business, fearing disease and the temptations of alcohol, as well as possible attacks by settlers along the way.

In order to cement the alliance, the British sent Colonial envoys who usually reported directly to the various provincial governors, one of whom was Benjamin Franklin, to the frontier and beyond. This decision helped win North America for the British—but only for a time. In the end, it still cost them the continent, or at least the better part of it. The Colonial delegates passed more than wampum over the council fires of the treaty summits. They also came home with an appetite for something that many proper colonials, and most proper British subjects, found little short of heresy. They returned with a taste for natural rights—life, liberty, and happiness—that they saw operating on the other side of the frontier. These observations would help mold the political life of the colonies, and much of the world, in the years to come.

CHAPTER THREE

"Our Indians Have Outdone the Romans"

The Five Nations have such absolute Notions of Liberty that they allow no kind of Superiority of one over another, and banish all Servitude from their Territories.

—Cadwallader Colden, 1727

By the mid–eighteenth century, when alliance with the Six Nations became an article of policy with the British Crown, English colonists had been living in North America for little more than a century. The colonies comprised a thin ribbon of settlement from a few miles north of Boston to a few miles south of Charleston. Barely a million people all told, the British colonists looked westward across mountains that seemed uncompromisingly rugged to English eyes, into the maw of a continent that they already knew was many times the size of their ancestral homeland. How much larger, no one at that time really knew. No one knew exactly how wide the forests might be, how far the rivers might reach, or what lay beyond them. There was a widespread belief that the Pacific Ocean lay out there, somewhere. The map makers settled for blank spaces and guesses.

Across the mountains were the homelands of Indian confederacies—the Iroquois to the northwest, the Cherokees to the Southwest, and others—which outnumbered the colonists and whose warriors had proved themselves tactically, if not technologically, equal to the British army on American ground. And there were the French, sliding southward along the spine of the mountains, establishing forts as close as Pittsburgh, their soldiers and trappers building the bases of empire along the rivers that laced the inland forests.

The British decision to seek the Iroquois' favor set in motion historical events that were to make North America a predominantly English-speaking continent. These events also, paradoxically, provided an opportunity for learning, observation, and reflection which in its turn gave the nation-to-be a character distinct from England and the rest of Europe, and which thus helped make the American Revolution possible.

The diplomatic approach to the Iroquois came at a time when the transplanted Europeans were first beginning to sense that they were something other than Europeans, or British subjects. Several generations had been born in the new land. The English were becoming, by stages, "Americans"—a word that had been reserved for Indians. From the days when the Puritans came to build their city on a hill there had been some feeling of distinction, but for a century most of the colonists had been escapees from Europe, or temporary residents hoping to extract a fortune from the new land and return, rich gentlemen all, to the homeland. After a century of settlement, however, that was changing.

From the days of Squanto's welcome and the first turkey dinner, the Indians had been contributing to what was becoming a new amalgam of cultures. In ways so subtle that they were often ignored, the Indians left their imprint on the colonists' eating habits, the paths they followed, the way they clothed themselves, and the way they thought. The Indians knew how to live in America, and the colonists, from the first settlers onward, had to learn.

When the British decided to send some of the colonies' most influential citizens to seek alliance with the Iroquois, the treaty councils that resulted provided more than an opportunity for diplomacy. They enabled the leading citizens of both cultures to meet and mingle on common and congenial ground, and thus to learn from each other. The pervasiveness and influence of these contacts has largely been lost in a history that, much like journalism, telescopes time into a series of conflicts—conquistadorial signposts on the way west.

Lost in this telescoping of history has been the intense fascination that the unfolding panorama of novelty that was America held for the new Americans—a fascination that was shipped eastward across the Atlantic to Spain, France, Britain, and Germany in hundreds of travel narratives, treaty accounts, and scientific treatises, in a stream that began with Columbus's accounts of the new world's wonders and persisted well into the nineteenth century.

The observations and reports that flooded booksellers of the time were often entirely speculative. Travel was very difficult, and what explorers could not reach, they often imagined. "A traveler' " wrote Benjamin Franklin in *Poor Richard* for 1737, "should have a hog's nose, a deer's legs and an ass's back"—testimony to the rugged nature and agonizingly slow pace of overland travel by stage or horse at a time when roads were virtually nonexistent outside of thickly settled areas, and when motorized transport was unknown. If crossing the ocean was an exercise in hardship, crossing the boundless continent was even more difficult. For the few people who did it (or tried) and who could read and write, there was a market: the boundaries of popular curiosity were as limitless as the continent seemed to be. That curiosity was matched by an equal array of ornate speculations on what lay beyond the next bend in this river or that, or beyond the crest of such and such a mountain. What new peoples were to be found?

What new and exotic plants and animals? Were there cities of gold? Mountains two miles high? Giants and Lilliputians? The speculations assumed a degree of vividness not unlike twentieth-century musings over the character of possible life on the planets.

The first systematic English-language account of the Iroquois' social and political system was published in 1727, and augmented in 1747, by Cadwallader Colden, who, in the words of Robert Waite, was regarded as "the best-informed man in the New World on the affairs of the British-American colonies." A son of Reverend Alexander Colden, a Scottish minister, Colden was born February 17, 1688, in Ireland. He arrived in America at age twenty-two, five years after he was graduated from the University of Edinburgh. Shortly after his arrival in America, Colden began more than a half century of service in various offices of New York Colonial government. His official career culminated in 1761 with an appointment as lieutenant governor of the colony. In addition to political duties, Colden carried on extensive research in natural science. He also became close to the Iroquois, and was adopted by the Mohawks.

In a preface to his *History of the Five Indian Nations Depending on the Province of New York in America*, Colden wrote that his account was the first of its kind in English:

> Though every one that is in the least acquainted with the affairs of North-America, knows of what consequence the Indians, commonly known to the people of New-York by the name of the Five Nations, are both in Peace and War, I know of no accounts of them published in English, but what are meer [sic] Translations of French authors.

Colden found the Iroquois to be "barbarians" because of their reputed tortures of captives, but he also saw a "bright and noble genius" in these Indians' "love of their country," which he compared to that of "the greatest Roman Hero's." "When Life and

[36]

Liberty came in competition, indeed, I think our Indians have outdone the Romans in this particular. . . . The Five Nations consisted of men whose Courage and Resolution could not be shaken." Colden was skeptical that contact with Euro-Americans could improve the Iroquois: "Alas! we have reason to be ashamed that these Infidels, by our Conversation and Neighborhood, have become worse than they were before they knew us. Instead of Vertues, we have only taught them Vices, that they were entirely free of before that time. The narrow Views of private interest have occasioned this."

Despite his condemnation of their reputed cruelty toward some of their captives, Colden wrote that Euro-Americans were imitating some of the Iroquois' battle tactics, which he described as the art of "managing small parties." The eastern part of the continent, the only portion of North America that the colonists of the time knew, was, in Colden's words, "one continued Forrest," which lent advantage to Iroquoian warfare methods. Such methods would later be put to work against British soldiers in the American Revolution.

Colden also justified his study within the context of natural science: "We are fond of searching into remote Antiquity to know the manners of our earliest progenitors; if I be not mistaken, the Indians are living images of them." The belief that American Indian cultures provided a living window on the prehistory of Europe was not Colden's alone. This assumption fueled curiosity about American Indian peoples on both sides of the Atlantic Ocean throughout the eighteenth century. Colden's was one of the first widely circulated observations of this sort, which compared Indians, especially the Iroquois, to the Romans and the Greeks, as well as other peoples such as the Celts and the Druids. Looking through this window on the past, it was believed that observation of Indian cultures could teach Europeans and Euro-Americans about the original form of their ancestors' societies—

those close to a state of nature that so intrigued the thought of the eighteenth-century Enlightenment, Colden, elaborating, wrote:

> The present state of the Indian Nations exactly shows the most Ancient and Original Condition of almost every Nation; so, I believe that here we may with more certainty see the original form of all government, than in the most curious Speculations of the Learned; and that the Patriarchal and other Schemes in Politicks are no better than Hypotheses in Philosophy, and as prejudicial to real Knowledge.

The original form of government, Colden believed, was similar to the Iroquois' system, which he described in some detail. This federal union, which Colden said "has continued so long that the Christians know nothing of the original of it," used public opinion extensively:

> Each nation is an absolute Republick by itself, govern'd in all Publick affairs of War and Peace by the Sachems of Old Men, whose Authority and Power is gained by and consists wholly in the opinions of the rest of the Nation in their Wisdom and Integrity. They never execute their Resolutions by Compulsion or Force Upon any of their People. Honour and Esteem are their principal Rewards, as Shame and being Despised are their Punishments.

The Iroquois' military leaders, like the civilian sachems, "obtain their authority . . . by the General Opinion of their Courage and Conduct, and lose it by a Failure in those Vertues," Colden wrote. He also observed that Iroquois leaders were generally regarded as servants of their people, unlike European kings, queens, and other members of a distinct hierarchy. It was customary, Colden observed, for Iroquois sachems to abstain from material things while serving their people, in so far as was possible:

Their Great Men, both Sachems [civil chiefs] and captains [war chiefs] are generally poorer than the common people, for they affect to give away and distribute all the Presents or Plunder they get in their Treaties or War, so as to leave nothing for themselves. If they should be once suspected of selfishness, they would grow mean in the opinion of their Country-men, and would consequently lose their authority.

Colden used the words of Monsieur de la Poterie, a French historian, to summarize his sentiments about the Iroquois' system of society and government:

When one talks of the Five Nations in France, they are thought, by a common mistake, to be meer Barbarians, always thirsting after human blood; but their True Character is very different. They are as Politick and Judicious as well can be conceiv'd. This appears from their management of the Affairs which they transact, not only with the French and the English, but likewise with almost all the Indian Nations of this vast continent.

Like Colden, French writers sometimes compared the Iroquois to the Romans. Three years before Colden published his *History of the Five Indian Nations Depending on the Province of New York in America* in its 1727 edition, a line drawing from a book by the Frenchman Joseph Francois Lafitau purported to illustrate an Iroquois council meeting. As was rather apparent from the drawing, the artist had never seen a meeting. In the drawing, a chief was shown standing, holding a wampum belt. He and other Iroquois sitting around him in a semicircle wore white, toga-like garments and sandals. Their hair was relatively short and curly, in the Roman fashion. The chiefs were shown sitting against a background that did not look at all like the American woodland, but more like the rolling, almost treeless Roman countryside. Accounts of Indian (especially Iroquoian) life and society, especially those by Colden, enjoyed a lively sale on both sides of the Atlantic.

Other eighteenth-century writers compared the Iroquois to counterparts of Old Testament life; James Adair's *History of the American Indians* (1775) "prefers simple Hebraic-savage honesty to complex British civilized corruption." Indians, wrote Adair, were governed by the "plain and honest law of nature . . . ":

> *Their whole constitution breathes nothing but liberty; and when there is equality of condition, manners and privileges, and a constant familiarity in society, as prevails in every Indian nation, and through all our British colonies, there glows such a cheerfulness and warmth of courage in each of their breasts, as cannot be described.*

Iroquoian notions of personal liberty also drew exclamations from Colden, who wrote:

> *The Five Nations have such absolute Notions of Liberty that they allow of no Kind of Superiority of one over another, and banish all Servitude from their Territories. They never make any prisoner a slave, but it is customary among them to make a Compliment of Naturalization into the Five Nations; and, considering how highly they value themselves above all others, this must be no small compliment . . .*

The Great Law provided for adoption of those prisoners willing to accept its provisions. For those who did not, there awaited the possible death by torture that Colden had deplored.

The Iroquois' extension of liberty and political participation to women surprised some eighteenth-century Euro-American observers. An unsigned contemporary manuscript in the New York State Library reported that when Iroquois men returned from hunting, they turned everything they had caught over to the women. "Indeed, every possession of the man except his horse & his rifle belong to the woman after marriage; she takes care of their Money and Gives it to her husband as she thinks his necessities require it," the unnamed observer wrote. The writer sought to refute assumptions that Iroquois women were "slaves of their husbands." "The truth is that Women are treated in a much more respectful manner than in England & that they possess a very superior power; this is to be attributed in a very great measure to their system of Education." The women, in addition to their political power and control of allocation from the communal stores, acted as communicators of culture between generations. It was they who educated the young.

Another matter that surprised many contemporary observers was the Iroquois' sophisticated use of oratory. Their excellence with the spoken word, among other attributes, often caused Colden and others to compare the Iroquois to the Romans and Greeks. The French use of the term Iroquois to describe the confederacy was itself related to this oral tradition; it came from the practice of ending their orations with the two words *hiro* and *kone*. The first meant "I say" or "I have said" and the second was an exclamation of joy or sorrow according to the circumstances of the speech. The two words, joined and made subject to French pronunciation, became Iroquois. The English were often exposed to the Iroquois' oratorical skills at eighteenth-century treaty councils.

Wynn R. Reynolds in 1957 examined 258 speeches by Iroquois at treaty councils between 1678 and 1776 and found that the speakers resembled the ancient Greeks in their primary emphasis on ethical proof. Reynolds suggested that the rich oratorical tradition may have been further strengthened by the exposure of children at an early age to a life in which oratory was prized and often heard.

More than curiosity about an exotic culture that was believed to be a window on a lost European past, drew Euro-Americans to the Iroquois. There were more immediate and practical concerns, such as the Iroquois' commanding military strength, their role in the fur trade, their diplomatic influence among other Indians and the Six Nations' geographical position astride the only relatively level pass between the mountains that otherwise separated British and French settlement in North America. During the eighteenth century, English Colonial settlement was moving inland, along the river valleys. Only a few hundred miles west of what was then the frontier outpost of Albany, the French were building forts north and west of the Great Lakes. The French, constantly at war with England during this period, were also penetrating the Mississippi Valley. Between the English and the French stood the Iroquois and their allies, on land that stretched, northeast to southwest, along nearly the entire frontier of the British colonies.

Before 1763, when the French were expelled from North America by the British and their Iroquois allies, the Six Nations enjoyed considerable diplomatic leverage, which was exploited with skill. The Iroquois' geographical position was important at a time when communication was limited to the speed of transportation, and the speed of transportation on land was limited to that of a man or woman on horseback. The Iroquois controlled the most logical transportation route between the coast and the interior, a route through which the Erie Canal was built in the early nineteenth century. Although the pass controlled by the Iroquois was relatively level compared to the land around it, the area was still thickly wooded. It was part of a wilderness that seemed so vast to the Euro-Americans that many of them assumed that Indians would always have a place in which to hunt, no matter how much of Europe's excess population crossed the Atlantic.

The rivalry between the British and French was on Colden's

mind as he wrote the introduction to the 1747 edition of his *History of the Five Indian Nations:*

> *The former part of this history was written at New-York in the year 1727, on Occasion of a Dispute which then happened, between the government of New-York and some Merchants. The French of Canada had the whole Fur Trade with the Western Indians in their Hands, and were supplied with their Woollen Goods from New-York. Mr. Burnet, who took more Pains to be Informed of the Interest of the People he was set over, and of making them useful to their Mother Country than Plantation Governors usually do, took the Trouble of Perusing all the Registers of the Indian Affairs on this occasion. He from thence conceived of what Consequences the Fur Trade with the Western Indians was of to Great Britain . . . the Manufactures depending on it.*

The Iroquois had not only the best route for trade and other transport, but also plenty of beaver. Colden recognized that to whom went the beaver might go the victory in any future war between France and Britain in North America. The mid–eighteenth century was a time when two nations could not join in battle unless they occupied neighboring real estate. The Iroquois' position indicated to Colden that their friendship, as well as business relations, must be procured if the English were to gain an advantage over the French:

> *He [Burnet] considered what influence this trade had on the numerous nations of Indians living on this vast continent of North America, and who surround the British Colonies; and what advantage it might be if they were influenced by the English in case of a war with France, and how prejudicial,*

on the other hand, if they were directed by the French Counsels.

The New York legislature soon recognized this reasoning, and acted to channel trade from the French to the English, Colden wrote. Such steps were not uncommon in the economic cold war between England and France during the middle of the century. The drawing up of sides that Colden advised was but another small step along the road to the final conflict in North America between these two European Colonial powers. As with the building of empires before and since the eighteenth century, trade and the flag often traveled in tandem, and economic conflict preceded overt military warfare. Robert Newbold (*The Albany Congress and Plan of Union*, 1955) assigned the competition for diminishing stocks of beaver a central role in the conflict between the British and French empires in North America during this period.

To Colden, trade with the Six Nations also presented an opportunity to mix and mingle with the Indians, and to convert them to the British Colonial interest:

> *I shall only add that Mr. Burnet's scheme had the desired effect: The English have gained the Trade which the French, before that, had with the Indians to the Westward of New York; and whereas, before that time, a very inconsiderable number of men were employed in the Indian Trade Abroad. Now above three hundred men are employed at the Trading House at Oswego alone, and the Indian trade has since that time yearly increased so far, that several Indian nations come now every summer to trade there, whose Names were not so much as known by the English before.*

As Colden had noted in his essay, the British were assembling a wide-ranging program of trade and diplomatic activity to insure that in any future war the Iroquois' powerful confederacy would side with them. Although, when the continent and its history are taken as a whole, the French were better at mixing with Indians and securing their alliance, at this particular time and in this place the English had the upper hand. This was accomplished through a series of adroit diplomatic moves, many of which were performed with the help of a group of men who, although English in background, were at home with the Iroquois as well.

The importance of the British alliance with the Iroquois was enhanced not only by the Six Nations' strategic position and military strength, but also by the Iroquois' diplomatic influence with many of the Indian nations of eastern North America. English and American writers remarked at the Iroquois' diplomatic and military power as early as 1687, when Governor Dongan of New York wrote that the Iroquois "go as far as the South Sea, the North West Passage and Florida to warr." The Iroquois did more than wage war; they were renowned in peacetime as traders, and as orators who traveled the paths that linked Indian nations together across most of eastern North America. When the English colonists had business with Indians in Ohio, and other parts of the Mississippi Valley, they often consulted the Iroquois. Clark Wissler classified many of the Indian nations situated around the Six Nations, including the Cherokees to the south, as members of the "Iroquois Family." The Iroquois' language was the language of diplomacy among Indians along much of the English Colonial frontier. These nations often contributed to, and borrowed from, practices of others. There is evidence that the Iroquoian form of government was imitated by other Indian nations.

One way that the English acted to maintain their alliance with the Iroquois, noted previously, was trade. The giving of gifts, an Indian custom, was soon turned by the English to their own ends. Gift giving was used by the English to introduce to Indians, and to invite their dependence on, the produce of England's embryonic industrial revolution. The English found it rather easy to outdo the French, whose industries were more rudimentary at the time, in gift giving. The Iroquois—premier military, political, and diplomatic figures on the frontier—were showered with gifts.

By 1744, the English effort was bearing fruit. At a treaty council during that year, Canassatego, the Iroquois chief, told Colonial commissioners from Pennsylvania, Maryland, and Virginia:

> *The Six Nations have a great Authority and Influence over the sundry tribes of Indians in alliance with the French, and Particularly the Praying Indians, formerly a part with ourselves, who stand in the very gates of the French, and to shew our further Care, we have engaged these very Indians, and other Indian allies of the French for you. They will not join the French against you. They have agreed with us before we set out. We have put the spirit of Antipathy against the French in those People. Our Interest is very Considerable with them, and many other [Indian] Nations, and as far as it ever extends, we shall use it for your service.*

During the 1744 treaty conference, the British commissioners traded with the Iroquois goods they held to be worth 220 pounds sterling and 15 shillings, including 200 shirts, four duffle blankets, forty-seven guns, one pound of vermillion, 1000 flints, four dozen Jews Harps, 202 bars of lead, two quarters shot, and two half-barrels of gun powder. The preponderance of military items indicated the strength of the alliance, and the expectation of hostilities with the French, against whom Canassatego had pledged the Iroquois' aid.

Although some of the older chiefs complained that the Indians ought to make do with their traditional clothes, foods, and weapons, the British gifts and trade items apparently were eagerly accepted. The accommodating English even established a separate gift-presentation ceremony for the chiefs, who were forbidden by the Great Law to take their share from the officially presented gifts until other tribal members had picked them over.

The English were not giving because they were altruistic; by showering the Iroquois with gifts, the English not only helped secure their alliance, but also made the Indians dependent on some of England's manufactures, thus creating new markets for the Crown. If, for example, the Iroquois took up European arms and laid down their traditional weapons, they also became dependent on a continuing supply of powder and lead. According to Jacobs, the British skillfully interwove the political and military objectives of imperialism with the economic objectives of mercantilism.

Much of the gift giving took place at treaty councils. Historically these meetings were some of the most important encounters of the century. By cementing an alliance with the Iroquois, the British were determining the course of the last in a series of Colonial wars with France in North America. The councils were conducted with solemnity befitting the occasion, a style that shows through their proceedings, which were published and widely read in the colonies and in Europe.

In the mid–eighteenth century, the only way to carry on serious diplomatic business was face to face. There were, of course, no telephones, no telegraph, and no shuttle diplomacy. Where it existed at all, mail service was slow, expensive, and often unreliable. It often took a letter as long to get from Boston to Charleston as from either city to London—at least a month, more likely six weeks, depending on the weather and other unpredictable circumstances.

On the English Colonial side of the table (or the council fire) sat such notables as Benjamin Franklin, his son William, William Johnson, Conrad Weiser, and Colden. The Iroquois' most eloquent sachems often spoke for the Six Nations, men such as Canassatego, Hendrick, and Shickallemy. These, and other lesser-known chiefs, were impressive speakers and adroit negotiators.

Canassatego was praised for his dignity and forcefulness of speech and his uncanny understanding of the whites. At the 1744 treaty council, Canassatego reportedly carried off "all honors in oratory, logical argument, and adroit negotiation," according to Witham Marshe, who observed the treaty council. Marshe wrote afterward that "Ye Indians seem superior to ye commissioners in point of sense and argument." His words were meant for Canassatego. An unusually tall man in the days when the average height was only slightly over five feet, Canassatego was well muscled, especially in the legs and chest, and athletic well past his fiftieth year. His size and booming voice, aided by a commanding presence gave him what later writers would call charisma—conversation stopped when he walked into a room. Outgoing to the point of radiance, Canassatego, by his own admission, drank too much of the white man's rum, and when inebriated was known for being unflatteringly direct in front of people he disliked. Because of his oratory, which was noted for both dignity and power, Canassatego was the elected speaker of the Grand Council at Onondaga during these crucial years.

Shickallemy was known among his own people as Swatane. As the Onondaga council's main liaison with the Shawnees, Conestogas, and Delawares, he was frequently in contact with the governments of Pennsylvania and New York, whose agents learned early that if they had business with these allied nations, they had business with Shickallemy, who handled their "European Affairs." Unlike many of the Iroquois chiefs, he was not a great orator. He was known for being a gentleman and a statesman—sensitive enough to deal with the Iroquois Indian allies, but also firm enough to deal with the whites beyond the frontier. In 1731, Governor Gordon of Pennsylvania gave to Shickallemy one of the first British Colonial messages seeking alliance against the French. In the swath of wooded hills that lay between the colonies and the governing seat of the Iroquois league, it was Shickallemy's sign— that of the turtle, his clan—that guaranteed safe passage to all travelers, British and Indian. In the Iroquoian language his name meant "the enlightener," and when he died in 1749, one year before Canassatego's death, word went out all through the country, on both sides of the frontier, that a lamp had gone out.

Shickallemy's life illustrated just how permeable the frontier could be during the eighteenth century. Born a Frenchman, he was taken prisoner at an early age by the Iroquois. He was later adopted by them and eventually elevated to membership in the Grand Council of the Confederacy as a pine-tree chief. Shickallemy, as an Iroquois chief, cultivated the friendship of the British colonists, and tried to pass this affection to his children, the youngest son of whom was Logan, who turned against the Euro-Americans only after most of his family was murdered by land squatters in 1774. Logan's speech after the murders was published by Jefferson in *Notes on the State of Virginia* and passed on, from there, to millions of nineteenth-century school children through *McGuffy's Readers.*

Hendrick's Iroquois name was Tiyanoga. Like Canassatego, he was described as one who could combine traditional Iroquoian dignity with forcefulness and brutal frankness when occasion called. The principal chief of the Mohawks, his warriors guarded the "eastern door" of the Iroquois longhouse, through which most diplomats and traders passed. Hendrick, like Canassatego, was described as an eloquent speaker. "No one equalled his force and eloquence," wrote Milton W. Hamilton. Hendrick, like some of the other chiefs, was fluent in English, but rarely spoke the language at treaty councils or in other contact with Euro-Americans. He apparently enjoyed eavesdropping on colonists' comments about the ignorant Indians who surely, they thought, couldn't understand what they were saying. Hendrick was a close friend of Sir

William Johnson; it was this relationship, more than any other individual bond, which kept the Iroquois allied with the English
until the French were expelled from the continent in 1763.

If it is surprising to find on the Indian side of the table sachems
bearing names usually associated with European nobles, it may be
just as surprising to find on the English side men who had absorbed so much of Indian life that they were at home on both
sides of the frontier. During the period when the English and Iroquois were allied, these men—English and Iroquois—mixed and
mingled freely, sitting in each other's councils, and living each
other's lives. Probably the most important Englishman on the
frontier was Sir William Johnson, Baronet. Johnson may have
been one of the men Franklin had in mind when he wrote that
English Colonial society had trouble maintaining its hold on
many men once they had tasted Indian life. An unidentified
friend of Johnson's wrote of him:

> *Something in his natural temper responds to Indian ways.*
> *The man holding up a spear he has just thrown, upon which*
> *a fish is now impaled; the man who runs, with his toes*
> *turned safely inward, through a forest where a greenhorn*
> *could not walk, the man sitting silent, gun on knee, in a*
> *towering black glade, watching by candle flame for the*
> *movement of antlers toward a tree whose bark has already*
> *been streaked by the tongues of deer; the man who can read*
> *a bent twig like an historical volume—this man is William*
> *Johnson, and he has learned all these skills from the Mo-*
> *hawks.* *

If Franklin was the most influential single individual at the Al-

---

* E. B. O'Callaghan, ed., John R. Brodhead, esq., *Documents Relative to the Colonial History of the State of New York* (Albany: Weed,
Parsons & Co., 1855), Vol. VI, p. 741.

bany congress, Johnson was not far behind. It was Johnson who persuaded the reluctant Iroquois to attend the congress, and who helped maintain an alliance that was often strained severely by conflicts over land, as well as the colonists' refusal to unite in face of the French threat. Johnson was characterized by the Mohawks at the Albany congress as "our lips and our tongue and our mouth." Johnson often dressed as an Iroquois, led war parties, sat on the Great Council of the league at times, and pursued Mohawk women relentlessly. His freelance sexual exploits were legend on both sides of the Atlantic; Johnson was said to have fathered a hundred Mohawk children. Such accounts have been disputed, but it is relatively certain that he fathered at least eight children among the Mohawks. The Mohawks did not seem to mind his fecundity; they did not worry about dilution of their gene pool because racial ethnocentricity was not widely practiced in Iroquoian culture. In fact, the Mohawks at the time appreciated Johnson's contributions because their population had been depleted by war, and since theirs was a matrilineal society, every child he bore became a Mohawk. The shade of one's skin meant less to the Mohawks than whether one accepted the laws of the Great Peace, which contained no racial bars to membership in the Six Nations.

Johnson's sexual exploits sometimes met with wry reproval from some of his white friends. Peter Wraxall, a former aide to Johnson, wrote to him after hearing that he was suffering from syphilis: "I thank God the pain in your breast is removed. I hope your cough will soon follow. As to the rest, you deserve the scourge and I won't say I pity you."

Johnson dealt extensively and maintained a close friendship with Colden. He also was a close friend of Hendrick, with whom he could speak fluent Iroquois. If the two men wished, they could also communicate in English, since Hendrick spoke it well, although he rarely spoke the language at treaty councils. The experiences of Johnson, who was at least as comfortable among the Iroquois as he was among the English (his knowledge of England came from Iroquois chiefs who had been there) illustrates how permeable the Anglo-Iroquois frontier was at this crucial juncture in Colonial history.

Perhaps the most important Pennsylvania colonial at the treaty councils was Conrad Weiser, a Mohawk by adoption who supplied many of the treaty accounts which Franklin published. A close friend of Franklin's, Weiser ranked with Johnson in the esteem given him by the Iroquois. Canassatego and Weiser were particularly close, and when the Iroquois adopted him, the sachem said that "we divided him into two parts. One we kept for ourselves, and one we left to you." He was addressing "Brother Onas," the Iroquoian name for the Pennsylvania Colonial governor. During the 1744 Lancaster treaty, Canassatego saluted Weiser:

> We hope that Tarachawagon [Weiser's Iroquois name] will
> be preserved by the good Spirit to a good old Age; when he
> is gone under Ground, it will be then time enough to look
> out for another, and no doubt that amongst so many Thou-
> sands as there are in the World, one such man may be
> found, who will serve both parties with the same Fidelity as
> Tarachawagon does; while he lives here there is no room to
> complain.

Weiser was the Iroquois' unofficial host at the 1744 Lancaster treaty. He bought them tobacco in hundred-pound sacks, found hats for many of the chiefs, and cracked jokes with Canassatego. Weiser also warned the colonists not to mock the Iroquois if they found the Indians' manners strange. He told the colonists that many of the Iroquois understood English, although they often pleaded ignorance of the language so that they could gather the colonists' honest appraisals of Indians and Indian society. When the Iroquois asked that rum-selling traders be driven from their lands, Weiser made a show by smashing some of the traders' kegs. When elderly Shickallemy became ill in 1747, Weiser dropped his official duties to care for the ailing sachem, and to make sure that blankets and food were delivered to his family during the winter.

The importance accorded treaty councils usually meant that the meetings would last at least two weeks, and sometimes longer. Most of the councils were held in the warmer season of the year, with June and July being the most favored months. It was during those months that oppressive heat and humidity enveloped the coastal cities and insects carried into them diseases such as malaria. It was a good time to retreat to the mountains—to Lancaster or Albany, or Easton, all frequent sites for treaty councils.

At treaty councils, leaders of both Indian and Euro-American cultures mingled not only at official meetings, but at convivial, off-the-record sessions as well. The atmosphere was that of a meeting of statesmen from co-equal nations, by most accounts an excellent atmosphere for the exchange of ideas of all kinds. This was especially true during the quarter-century before 1763, when the Crown's need for Iroquois alliance enforced a respect for cultural practices that some of the more ethnocentric Colonial commissioners found distasteful. The treaty councils were the primary means not only for maintaining the Anglo-Iroquois alliance against the French, but for addressing matters, such as illegal land squatting, which often strained the alliance. Appeals by the Indians for Colonial commissioners to control the activities of their own citizens were standard fare at the opening of most treaty councils. Once such problems had been addressed, the parties got down to diplomacy. "Shining the covenant chain" was the metaphor most often used at the time for such activity.

The tone of the treaty councils was that of a peer relationship; the leaders of sovereign nations met to address mutual problems.

The dominant assumptions of the Enlightenment, near its height during the mid–eighteenth century, cast Indians as equals in intellectual abilities and moral sense to the progressive Euro-American minds of the time. It was not until the nineteenth century that expansionism brought into its service the full flower of systematic racism that defined Indians as children, or wards, in the eyes of Euro-American law, as well as popular discourse.

Interest in treaty accounts was high enough by 1736 for a Philadelphia printer, Benjamin Franklin, to begin publication and distribution of them. During that year, Franklin published his first treaty account, recording the proceedings of a meeting in his home city during September and October of that year. During the next twenty-six years, Franklin's press produced thirteen treaty accounts. During those years, Franklin became involved to a greater degree in the Indian affairs of Pennsylvania. By the early 1750s, Franklin was not only printing treaties, but representing Pennsylvania as an Indian commissioner as well. It was his first diplomatic assignment. Franklin's attention to Indian affairs grew in tandem with his advocacy of a federal union of the colonies, an idea that was advanced by Canassatego and other Iroquois chiefs in treaty accounts published by Franklin's press as early as 1744. Franklin's writings indicate that as he became more deeply involved with the Iroquois and other Indian peoples, he picked up ideas from them concerning not only federalism, but concepts of natural rights, the nature of society and man's place in it, the role of property in society, and other intellectual constructs that would be called into service by Franklin as he and other American revolutionaries shaped an official ideology for the new United States. Franklin's intellectual interaction with Indian peoples began, however, while he was a Philadelphia printer who was helping to produce what has since been recognized as one of the few indigenous forms of American literature to be published during the Colonial period. In the century before the American Revolution, some fifty treaty accounts were published, covering forty-five treaty councils. Franklin's press produced more than a quarter of the total. These documents were one indication that a group of colonies occupied by transplanted Europeans were beginning to develop a new sense of themselves; a sense that they were not solely European, but American as well.

Benjamin Franklin was one of a remarkable group who helped transform the mind of a group of colonies that were becoming a nation. It would be a nation that combined the heritages of two continents—that of Europe, their ancestral home, and America, the new home in which their experiment would be given form and expression.

CHAPTER FOUR

Such an Union

It would be a very strange thing if Six Nations of Ignorant Savages should be capable of forming a Scheme for such an Union and be able to execute it in such a manner, as that it has subsisted Ages, and appears indissoluble, and yet a like Union should be impracticable for ten or a dozen English colonies.
—Benjamin Franklin to James Parker, 1751

By 1744, Benjamin Franklin had lived in Philadelphia little more than two decades. Having fled what he regarded as Boston's spirit-crushing Puritan orthodoxy, Franklin's iconoclastic wit found a more comfortable home in Quaker Philadelphia. The city was only a quarter century old when Franklin arrived at the age of seventeen, a dirty, penniless young man looking for work as a printer's apprentice. During the two decades between his 1723 arrival and 1744, Franklin not only found work, but set up his own press, and prospered along with the Quaker capital. With 10,000 residents and a fertile hinterland much larger and more productive than Boston's, young Philadelphia already was approaching the older city in size.

By 1744, his thirty-eighth year, Franklin had a thriving printing business that published one of the largest newspapers in the colonies, the *Pennsylvania Gazette*, as well as *Poor Richard's Almanack*, which appeared annually. As the province's official printer, Franklin ran off his press all of Pennsylvania's paper money, state documents and laws, as well as job printing. As the postmaster, he had free access to the mails to distribute his publications. If a family, especially a Pennsylvania family, kept printed matter other than the Bible in the house, it was very likely that whatever it was—newspaper, almanac or legal documents—bore Franklin's imprint.

Franklin had done more for Philadelphia than fill its book stalls (one of which he owned) with literature. He had helped clean the city's streets and construct a drainage system unparalleled in its time; he had helped form a city fire department, a hospital, and a library; he would soon be testing electricity, and was already thinking of how it might be used for household lighting. While he detested religious orthodoxy (especially the Puritan variety) he shared one Puritan attribute with the merchants of young, bustling Philadelphia. He believed that hard work warmed God's heart or, as he wrote in *Poor Richard* for 1736: "God helps those who help themselves."

Like any publisher of ambition, Franklin always kept a sharp eye out for salable properties. During 1736, he had started printing small books containing the proceedings of Indian treaty councils. The treaties, one of the first distinctive forms of indigenous American literature, sold quite well, which pleased Franklin. Filling the seemingly insatiable appetite for information about the Indians and the lands in which they lived that existed at the time on both sides of the Atlantic, Franklin's press turned out treaty accounts until 1762 when, journeying to England to represent Pennsylvania in the royal court, he found several English publishers in competition with him.

One warm summer day in 1744, Franklin was balancing the books of his printing operation when Conrad Weiser, the Indian interpreter and envoy to the Iroquois, appeared at his door with a new treaty manuscript—the official transcript of the recently completed meeting between envoys from Pennsylvania, Virginia, Maryland, and the sachems of the Six Nations confederacy at nearby Lancaster. Weiser, an old friend of Franklin's, explained that this was probably the most interesting and noteworthy treaty account he had ever brought in for publication. At last, said Weiser, the Iroquois had made a definite commitment toward the Anglo-Iroquois alliance that Pennsylvania and other Colonial governments had been seeking for more than ten years.

The Iroquois, explained Weiser, were being careful. If they were to ally with the English, they wanted the colonials to unify their management of the Indian trade, and to do something about the crazy patchwork of diplomacy that resulted when each colony handled its own affairs with the Iroquois.

Taking the handwritten manuscript from Weiser, Franklin sat at his desk and quickly thumbed through it, reading a few passages, bringing to life in his mind the atmosphere of the frontier council. The treaty had two main purposes, Franklin surmised. The first was to deal with a recurring problem: Indian complaints that Englishmen, mostly Scotch-Irish frontiersmen, were moving onto Indian land without permission, disrupting hunting and social life. The second, and more important, objective was to polish the covenant chain, to secure the alliance against the French.

The Iroquois party consisted of 245 chiefs, warriors, women, and children. Weiser met the party outside Lancaster, throwing his arms around his friend Canassatego who, at age sixty, was entering his last years as speaker of the great council at Onondaga. Weiser bid all the Iroquois welcome to Pennsylvania, joking in the Iroquois language with the chiefs, who counted him as one of their own, an adopted Mohawk who often traveled to Onondaga to sit in on the councils of the league.

Weiser knew that the Iroquois expected their protocol to be

followed. As guests, this meant that they had a right to adequate food and lodging after the long and tiring trip. Weiser promptly ordered a steer killed for them. While the steer was being carved into steaks, he purchased 300 pounds of flour, as well as other provisions, charging all of it to the provincial government. He treated the chiefs to "a glass of rum," and then another. The chiefs, "desireous . . . to have one more dram which I could not deny them," asked for more, and Weiser again bought drinks all around. The next day, he entered on his expense ledger a half-dozen sheep, 250 pounds of flour, bread, and "other necessities."

The Iroquois delegates arrived at Lancaster's courthouse Friday, June 22, 1744. A group of Colonial delegates, led by George Thomas, Esq., were waiting with "Wine, Punch, Pipes and Tobacco." The Colonial delegates "drank to the health of the Six Nations" and then adjourned the meeting until Monday to give the Iroquois an opportunity to rest.

For most of the next two weeks, the Iroquois and Colonial delegates discussed the invasion by squatters of the eastern slopes of the Appalachians. The delegates from Maryland and Virginia attended because both colonies claimed the land in question. Governor Thomas opened the first business session of the council Monday, June 25, by observing that during a treaty council at Philadelphia two years earlier, the Iroquois had requested a meeting with the governors of Maryland and Virginia "concerning some lands in the back parts of [those] Provinces which they claim a right to from their Conquests over the Ancient Possessors, and which have been settled by some of the Inhabitants of those Governments [Maryland and Virginia] without their [Iroquois'] consent, or any purchase made from them." Thomas reported that "an unfortunate skirmish" had taken place between colonists' militia and war parties from the Six Nations in the disputed territory. Thomas asserted that this problem ought to be solved because the Iroquois were strategic to the British defense against the French in North America: "by their Situation . . . if Friends [the Iroquois] are capable of defending [Colonial] settlements; if enemies, of making cruel Ravages upon them; if Neuters, they may deny the French a passage through their country and give us timely Notice of their designs."

The representatives of Maryland were not as conciliatory as Thomas. Speaking to the Iroquois, they said:

> *The Great King of England, and his Subjects, have always possessed the Province of Maryland free and undisturbed from any Claim by the Six Nations for above one hundred Years past, and your not saying anything to us before, convinces us you thought you had no Pretence to any land in Maryland; nor can we yet find out to what Lands, or under what Title you make your Claim.*

The Iroquois waited a day, until June 26, to reply, as was their custom. The day's delay was meant to signal grave concern over the issue at hand. In some cases, the delay was just a matter of being polite; in this case, however, it was sincere. On Tuesday afternoon, Canassatego rose before the assembly, assuming the posture that had caused many colonists to compare him to their imagined Roman and Greek ancestors. He said:

> *Brother, the Governor of Maryland,*
> *When you mentioned the Affair of the Land Yesterday, you went back to Old Times, and told us that you had been in Possession of the Province of Maryland for above one hundred Years; but what is one hundred Years in comparison to the length of Time since our Claim began? Since we came out of this ground? For we must tell you that long before one hundred years our Ancestors came out of this very ground, and their children have remained here ever*

*since. . . . You came out of the ground in a country that lies
beyond the Seas; there you may have a just Claim, but here
you must allow us to be your elder Brethren, and the lands
to[o] belong[ed] to us before you knew anything of them.*

Canassatego continued his argument, saying that some Europeans
assumed, in error, that the Indians would have perished "if they
had not come into the country and furnished us with Strowds and
Hatchets, and Guns, and other things necessary for the support of
Life." The Indians, the sachem reminded the colonists, "lived before they came amongst us, and as well, or better, if we may believe what our forefathers have taught us. We had then room
enough, and plenty of Deer, which was easily caught."

By July 2, the Iroquois had been given vague assurances by the
Colonial commissioners that the flow of settlers into the disputed
lands would be controlled as much as possible, a promise the Colonial officials did not have the armed force to implement. A few
other matters that had precipitated conflict between the Iroquois
and the English, such as the murder of Indian trader John Armstrong by the Delawares, were discussed. As the treaty council entered its last few days, talk turned to cementing the alliance, shining the covenant chain. Canassatego assured the Colonial
delegates that "we will take all the care we can to prevent an
enemy from coming onto British lands." To insure the contin-
uance of alliance, the sachem also suggested that the colonists put
their own house in order by combining into a single federal union.
Closing his final speech on July 4, 1744, Canassatego told the assembled Iroquois and colonial commissioners:

*Our wise forefathers established union and amity between
the Five Nations. This has made us formidable. This has
given us great weight and authority with our neighboring
Nations. We are a powerful Confederacy and by your ob-*

[61]

serving the same methods our wise forefathers have taken you will acquire much strength and power; therefore, whatever befalls you, do not fall out with one another.*

Governor Thomas's final response, which followed Canassatego's, did not mention the sachems' proposal that the colonies unite into a confederacy on the Iroquoian model. Thomas also seemed to have missed Canassatego's assertion on June 26 that the colonists ought to consider the Iroquois their elder brethren. "We are all subjects, as well as you, of the great King beyond the Water," Thomas said. The Iroquois, following their custom of granting each speaker his say without interruption, did not dispute Thomas's assertion, although Canassatego had made it clear that they did not submit to the king's authority. The Iroquois regarded themselves as independent, beholden to no European power. They were, in fact, courted eagerly during the two decades before 1763 by both England and France.

The 1744 treaty, one of the more dramatic during this period, impressed Franklin when the interpreter's record was delivered to him a few weeks later. He printed 200 extra copies and sent them to England. Within three years after he printed the proceedings of the 1744 treaty, with Canassatego's advice on Colonial union, Franklin became involved with Cadwallader Colden on the same subject. A new edition of Colden's *History of the Five Indian Nations Depending on the Province of New York in America*, first published in 1727, was issued during 1747. Franklin was a frequent correspondent with Colden at this time; both had similar interests in politics, natural science, and Deism. They got on together well and often until 1765 when Colden, then lieutenant

---

* This quotation and the associated narrative describing the 1744 treaty council is based on Franklin's account, published in Carl Van Doren and Julian P. Boyd, eds., *Indian Treaties Printed by Benjamin Franklin* (Philadelphia: Pennsylvania Historical Society, 1938).

governor of New York, was burned in effigy for enforcing the Stamp Act.

Shortly after its publication in 1747, Franklin asked Colden for a copy of his new edition, and read and appraised it for its author. Franklin then began his own fervent campaign for a federal union of the British colonies, a cause he did not forsake until the United States was formed a quarter-century later.

Franklin requested a copy of Colden's book at a time when alliance with the Iroquois was assuming a new urgency for Pennsylvania. During 1747, French and Dutch privateers had raided along the Delaware River, threatening Philadelphia itself for a time. In response, Franklin organized a volunteer militia that elected its own officers (a distinctly Iroquoian custom). The militia grew year by year, repeatedly electing Franklin its colonel until the British, worried about the growth of indigenous armed forces in the colonies, ordered it disbanded in 1756.

Franklin thought enough of Colden's history to ask for fifty copies to sell through his own outlets. Franklin did not, however, approve of the fact that the book had been "puffed up" with "the Charters &c of this Province, all under the Title of the *History of the Five Nations.*" Franklin deplored such padding, which he called "a common Trick of Booksellers." Such puffery notwithstanding, Franklin was concerned that one bookseller, by the name of Read, was not giving Colden's work sufficient advertising in Philadelphia. "In our last two Papers he has advertis'd generally that he has a parcel of books to sell, Greek, Latin, French and English, but makes no particular mention of the Indian History; it is therefore no wonder that he has sold none of them, as he told me a few days since." Franklin complained that no one in Philadelphia except himself had read the book, and he thought it "well wrote, entertaining and instructive" and "useful to all those colonies who have anything to do with Indian Affairs."

As early as 1750, Franklin recognized that the economic and

political interests of the British colonies were diverging from those of the mother country. About the same time, he began to think of forms of political confederation that might suit a dozen distinct, often mutually suspicious, political entities. A federal structure such as the Iroquois Confederacy, which left each state in the union to manage its own internal affairs and charged the confederate government with prosecuting common, external matters, must have served as an expedient, as well as appealing, example. As Franklin began to express his thoughts on political and military union of the colonies, he was already attempting to tie them together culturally, through the establishment of a postal system and the American Philosophical Society, which drew to Philadelphia the premier Euro-American scholars of his day.

During 1751, Franklin read a pamphlet written by Archibald Kennedy titled "The Importance of Gaining and Preserving the Friendship of the Indians to the British Interest Considered." Kennedy, collector of customs and receiver general for the province of New York at the time that he wrote the brochure, maintained that alliance with the Iroquois was "of no small importance to the trade of Great Britain, as to the peace and prosperity of the colonies." Indian traders, called "a tribe of harpies" by Kennedy, "have so abused, defrauded and deceived those poor, innocent, well-meaning people." Kennedy asserted that fraud in the Indian trade could be reduced if that trade were regulated through a single Indian commissioner, instead of a different one for each colony, which was the existing system. As with Kennedy, so also with the Iroquois; they too much resented the behavior of the traders. Canassatego had told the Colonial commissioners at Lancaster in 1744 that the Indians would be poor "as long as there are too many Indian traders among us." Resolution of this problem was the key to maintaining the Anglo-Iroquois alliance in Kennedy's opinion. The appointment of a single Indian commissioner would also be a small step along the road to Colonial confederation for mutual defense. The Iroquois had been advocating a unified Colonial military command for at least seven years—since Canassatego's speech to the 1744 Lancaster treaty. Under Kennedy's scheme, each colony would have contributed men and money to the common military force in proportion to its population.

Franklin was sent Kennedy's brochure by James Parker, his New York City printing partner, from whose press it had been issued. Following the reading of the brochure, Franklin cultivated Kennedy's friendship; the two men consulted together on the Albany Plan of Union (which included Kennedy's single-Indian agent idea). At the Albany congress itself, Franklin called Kennedy "a gentleman of great knowledge in Public Affairs."

After he read Kennedy's brochure, Franklin wrote to Parker that "I am of the opinion, with the public-spirited author, that securing the Friendship of the Indians is of the greatest consequence for these Colonies." To Franklin, "the surest means of doing it are to regulate the Indian Trade, so as to convince them [the Indians] that they may have the best and cheapest Goods, and the fairest dealings, with the English." Franklin also thought, in agreement with Kennedy, that the colonists should accept the Iroquois' advice to form a union in common defense under a common, federal government:

> And to unite the several Governments as to form a strength
> that the Indians may depend on in the case of a Rupture
> with the French, or apprehend great Danger from, if they
> break with us. This union of the colonies, I apprehend, is
> not to be brought about by the means that have heretofore
> been used for that purpose.

Franklin then asked why the colonists found it so difficult to unite in common defense, around common interests, when the Iroquois had done so long ago. In context, his use of the term "ignorant savages" seems almost like a backhanded slap at the colonists, who may have thought themselves superior to the Indians but who, in Franklin's opinion, could learn something from the Six Nations about political unity:

> *It would be a very strange thing if Six Nations of Ignorant Savages should be capable of forming a Scheme for such an Union and be able to execute it in such a manner, as that it has subsisted Ages, and appears indissoluble, and yet a like union should be impracticable for ten or a dozen English colonies.*

Within a year of reading Kennedy's brochure, Franklin, whose role in Pennsylvania's Indian affairs was growing, prepared a report on the expenses of the province's Indian agents. Part of the report was sharply critical of Indian traders:

> *Some very unfit Persons are at present employed in that business [the Indian trade]. We hope that the Governor will enjoin the justices of the County Courts to be more careful in the future whom they recommend for Licenses; and whatever is thought further necessary to enforce the Laws now being, for regulating the Indian Trade and Traders, may be considered by the ensuing Assembly. . . .*

Recognizing that the Indians' complaints about the conduct of English traders had to be addressed if the Anglo-Iroquois alliance was to be maintained, Franklin took a major step in his personal life. During 1753 Franklin, who had heretofore only printed Indian treaties, accepted an appointment by the Pennsylvania government as one of the colony's commissioners at a meeting with the Six Nations planned for later that year in Carlisle.

That appointment was no more than an official recognition of what had already become obvious. Franklin had gradually emerged as an important part of the British diplomatic offensive with the Iroquois, an offensive that grew in activity until the conclusion of the war with France in 1763. Pennsylvania alone spent 1259 pounds, 5 shillings, 11 pence on Indian affairs during 1750, and about the same amount in 1751. Expenditures on Indian affairs had increased from 13 pounds in 1734 to 143 pounds in 1735, and 303 pounds in 1744, the year of the Lancaster treaty council during which Canassatego issued his challenge to the colonies to unite. These figures indicate that Franklin, Kennedy, and Colden were not alone in their insistence that an alliance with the Iroquois and other Indians along the Northern frontier was important to the security of the British colonies as against the French.

During the year before Franklin attended his first treaty council in an official capacity, the possibility of conflict with the French was accentuated by a French advance into the Ohio Valley. During June 1752, French troops attacked the Indian town of Pickawillany. The Pennsylvania Assembly voted 800 pounds in aid for the attacked Indians, 600 of which was earmarked for "necessities of life," a euphemism for implements of war. The French continued to advance during the balance of the year; French forces probed deeper into the territories of Indians allied with the Iroquois, the allies to whom Canassatego had referred in his final speech at the 1744 treaty conference. French forts were erected at Presque Isle, Le Boeuf, and Venango.

James Hamilton's proclamation appointing Franklin, Richard Peters, and Issac Norris to treat with the Indians at Carlisle specifically mentioned the alliance with the Twightwees, allies of the Iroquois who lived in the Ohio Valley, and who had been attacked by the French during 1752. The treaty, which started Franklin's distinguished diplomatic career, began November 1, 1753. An account of the treaty was printed and sold by Franklin's press. The major subject of the Carlisle treaty was mutual defense against the French. The Indians also brought up the behavior of traders, especially regarding their distribution of rum among Indians. The chiefs said they wanted such practices stopped. Scarrooyady, an Iroquois who had assumed a leadership role following the death of Canassatego during 1750, told the commissioners:

> *Your traders now bring us scarce any Thing but Rum and Flour. They bring us little Powder and Lead, or other valuable Goods. The rum ruins us. We beg you would prevent its coming in such Quantities, by regulating the Traders. . . . We desire it be forbidden, and none sold in the Indian Country.*

"Those wicked Whiskey Sellers, when they have once got the Indians in Liquor, make them sell their very Clothes from their Backs," Scarrooyady emphasized. Concluding their report to the provincial government on the treaty council, Franklin, Peters, and Norris advised that the sachem's advice be taken. "That the traders are under no Bonds . . . and by their own Intemperance, unfair Dealings and Irregularities will, it is to be feared, entirely estrange the affections of the Indians from the English." Franklin's opposition to the liquor trade was strengthened the night following the formal conclusion of the treaty council, when many of the Indians there became very drunk and disorderly, yielding to the addictive qualities of the liquids that their chiefs had deplored only a few days earlier.

Two stated desires of the Iroquois leadership—that the Indian trade be regulated along with the illegal movement of settlers into the interior, and that the colonies form a federal union—figured importantly in Franklin's plans for the Albany congress of 1754. Plans for this, the most important intercolonial conference in the years before the last North American war with France, were being made at the time of the Carlisle treaty conference. The London Board of Trade wrote to the New York provincial government September 18, 1753, directing all the colonies that had dealings with the Iroquois to join in "one general Treaty to be made in his Majesty's name." It was a move that began, in effect, to bring about the unified management of Indian affairs that Colden, Kennedy, Franklin, and the Iroquois had requested. Similar letters were sent to all colonies that shared frontiers with the Iroquois and their Indian allies, from Virginia northward. Franklin was appointed to represent Pennsylvania at the Albany congress.

The congress convened June 19, 1754, five days after its scheduled opening because many of the Iroquois and some of the Colonial commissioners arrived late. Sessions of the congress, as well as some meetings with the Iroquois delegations, took place at the Albany courthouse, in the midst of a town that straddled the frontier between the English and the Mohawks, who maintained the "eastern door" of the Iroquois longhouse. Albany at the time was still dominated by the architecture of the Dutch, who had started the town before the English replaced them.

The Albany congress met for two interconnected reasons: to cement the alliance with the Iroquois against the French and to formulate and ratify a plan of union for the colonies. Franklin, well known among the Indians and a fervent advocate of Colonial union, was probably the most influential individual at the congress.

Among the Iroquois who attended the congress, Hendrick, who was called Tiyanoga among the Iroquois, received a special invitation from James de Lancy, acting governor of New York, to provide information on the structure of the Iroquois Confederacy to the Colonial delegates. De Lancy, appointed as chief executive of the congress by the Crown, met Saturday, June 29, with Hendrick and other Iroquois sachems. During that meeting, Hendrick held a chain belt that had been given him by the Colonial delegates. He made of the belt a metaphor for political union. "So we will use our endeavors to add as many links to it as lyes within our

[69   ]

power," Hendrick said. "In the meantime we desire that you will strengthen yourselves, and bring as many into this Covenant Chain as you possibly can."

During the evening of July 8, the Iroquois' last in Albany, de Lancy met again with Hendrick and other Iroquois. During this meeting, which was open to the public, Hendrick remarked (as had Canassatego ten years earlier) about the strength that confederation brought the Iroquois. De Lancy replied: "I hope that by this present [Plan of] Union, we shall grow up to a great height and be as powerful and famous as you were of old." The week before this exchange, the final draft of Franklin's plan of union had been approved by delegates to the congress, after extensive debate.

Debates over the plan had taken more than two weeks. On June 24, the Colonial delegates voted without dissent in support of Colonial union that, said the motion voted on, "[is] absolutely necessary for their [the colonies'] security and defense." A committee was appointed to "prepare and receive Plans or Schemes for the Union of the Colonies." Franklin was a member of that committee. Thomas Hutchinson, a delegate from Massachusetts who also served on the committee, later pointed to Franklin as the major contributor to the plan of union that emerged from the deliberations of the committee: "The former [the Albany plan] was the projection of Dr. F[ranklin] and prepared in part before he had any consultation with Mr. H[utchinson], probably brought with him from Philadelphia."

Franklin had drawn up "Short Hints Toward a Scheme for Uniting the Northern Colonies," which he mailed to Colden and James Alexander for comment June 8, 1754, eleven days before the Albany congress opened. The committee on which Franklin and Hutchinson sat developed its own set of "short hints" by June 28, four days after its first meeting. This list was basically similar to, and appears to have developed from, Franklin's own list.

Delegates to the Albany congress debated the committee's "short hints" on eight occasions between de Lancy's two meetings with Hendrick. On July 9, the Iroquois having left town, Franklin was asked to draw up a plan of union based on the previous two weeks' discussions. Franklin's final draft was commissioned two weeks to the day after his *Pennsylvania Gazette* published the "Join or Die" cartoon, one of the first graphic editorials to appear in an American newspaper, and a forceful statement in favor of Colonial union.

During debates over the plan of union, Franklin cited Kennedy's brochure and pointed to "the strength of the League which has bound our Friends the Iroquois together in a common tie which no crisis, however grave, since its foundation has managed to disrupt." Recalling the words of Hendrick, Franklin stressed the fact that the individual nations of the confederacy managed their own internal affairs without interference from the Grand Council. "Gentlemen," Franklin said, peering over the spectacles he had invented, "I propose that all the British American colonies be federated under a single legislature and a president-general to be appointed by the Crown." He then posed the same rhetorical question he had in the letter to Parker: if the Iroquois can do it, why can't we?

The plan of union that emerged from Franklin's pen was a skillful diplomatic melding of concepts that took into consideration the Crown's demands for control, the colonists' desires for autonomy in a loose union, and the Iroquois' stated advocacy of a Colonial union similar to theirs in structure and function. For the Crown, the plan provided administration by a president–general, to be appointed and supported by the Crown. The individual colonies were promised that they could retain their own constitutions "except in the particulars wherein a change may be directed by the said Act [the plan of union] as hereafter follows."

The retention of internal sovereignty within the individual colonies, politically necessary because of their diversity, geographical separation, and mutual suspicion, closely resembled the Iroquoian system. The colonies' distrust of one another and the fear of the smaller that they might be dominated by the larger in a confederation may have made necessary the adoption of another Iroquoian device: one colony could veto the action of the rest of the body. As in the Iroquois Confederacy, all "states" had to agree on a course of action before it could be taken. Like the Iroquois Great Council, the "Grand Council" (the name was Franklin's) of the colonies under the Albany Plan of Union would have been allowed to choose its own speaker. The Grand Council, like the Iroquois Council, was to be unicameral, unlike the two-house British system. Franklin favored one-house legislatures during and later at the Constitutional Convention, and opposed the imposition of a bicameral system on the United States.

Franklin's Albany Plan of Union provided for a different number of representatives from each colony (from seven for Virginia and Massachusetts Bay to two for New Hampshire and Rhode Island) as the Iroquois system provided for differing numbers from each of its five nations. This division of seats was based, however, in rough proportion to population and contributions to a common military force, while the Iroquois system was based more on tradition. But the number of delegates to the proposed Colonial Grand Council (forty-eight) closely resembled that of the Iroquois Council (fifty). There is no documentary evidence, however, that Franklin intended such a slavish imitation.

The legislature under the Albany plan was empowered to "raise and pay Soldiers, and build Forts for the Defence of any of the Colonies, and equip vessels of Force to guard the Coasts and protect the Trade on the Oceans, Lakes and Great Rivers," but it was not allowed to "impress men in any Colonies without the consent of its Legislature." This clause strikes a middle ground between the involuntary conscription often practiced in Europe at the time and the traditional reliance of the Iroquois and many other American Indian nations on voluntary military service.

The Albany plan also contained the long-sought unified regulation of the Indian trade advocated by the Iroquois, Kennedy, Colden, and Franklin:

> *That the President General with the advice of the Grand Council hold and direct all Indian Treaties in which the general interest or welfare of the Colonys may be concerned; and make peace or declare war with the Indian Nations. That they make such laws as they judge necessary for regulating Indian Trade. That they make all purchases from the Indians for the Crown. . . . That they make new settlements on such purchases by granting lands. . . .*

The last part of this section aimed to stop, or at least slow, the pellmell expansion of the frontier that resulted in settlers' occupation of lands unceded by the Indian nations. Such poaching was a constant irritant to the Iroquois; the subject of land seizures had come up at every treaty council for at least two decades before the Albany plan was proposed. Like the traders' self-interested profiteering, the illegal taking of land by frontiersmen was seen by Anglo-American leaders as a threat to the Anglo-Iroquois alliance at a time when worsening diplomatic relations with France made alliance with the Iroquois more vital.

The Albany Plan of Union gained Franklin general recognition in the colonies as an advocate of Colonial union. The plan also earned Franklin a position among the originators of the federalist system of government that came to characterize the United States political system. According to Clinton Rossiter, "Franklin made rich contributions to the theory and practice of federalism . . . he was far ahead of the men around him in abandoning provincialism."* While the Iroquois and Franklin were ready for a Colonial union, the legislatures of the colonies were not. Following its passage by the Albany congress on July 10, 1754, Franklin's plan died in the Colonial legislatures. The individual colonies' governing bodies were not ready to yield even to the limited Colonial government that Franklin proposed within his definition of federalism: "Independence of each other, and separate interests, tho' among a people united by common manners, language and, I may say, religion . . ." Franklin showed his dismay at the inability of the colonies to act together when he said that "the councils of the savages proceeded with better order than the British Parliament."

Franklin believed, at the time that his plan failed to win the approval of the colonies, that its defeat would cost the British their alliance with the Iroquois. "In my opinion, no assistance from them [the Six Nations] is to be expected in any dispute with the French 'till by a Compleat Union among our selves we are able to support them in case they should be attacked," Franklin wrote, before the Iroquois' willingness to maintain the alliance proved him wrong. Although he was wrong in this regard, Franklin's statement illustrates how important the Iroquois' prodding was in his advocacy of a federal union for the colonies.

Franklin's plan was also rejected by the Crown, but for reasons different from those of the Colonial legislatures. To the British, the plan was too democratic. It gave the colonists too much freedom at a time when the British were already sending across the ocean spies who reported that far too many colonists were giving entirely too much thought to possible independence from Britain. Franklin already was under watch as a potential troublemaker (hadn't he raised his own militia?).

The separate Colonial governments and the Crown had, in ef-

---

* Clinton Rossiter, *Seedtime of the Republic: The Origin of the Tradition of Political Liberty* (New York: Harcourt, Brace & Co., 1953), p. 306.

fect, vetoed the plan of the Albany commissioners—a veto beyond which there could be no appeal. Nonetheless, the work of the congress was not in vain.

Almost two decades would pass before the colonists—inflamed into union by the Stamp Act and other measures the British pressed upon the colonies to help pay the Crown's war debts—would take Franklin's and Canassatego's advice, later epitomized in Franklin's phrase: "We must all hang together or assuredly we shall all hang separately." Returning to America from one of many trips to England, Franklin would then repackage the Albany plan as the Articles of Confederation. A Continental Congress would convene, and word would go out to Onondaga that the colonists had finally lit their own Grand Council fire at Philadelphia.

During 1774, colonists dressed as Mohawks dumped tea into Boston Harbor to protest British economic imperialism. During the spring of 1775, serious skirmishes took place at Lexington and Concord. During August of the same year, commissioners from the newly united colonies met with chiefs of the Six Nations at Philadelphia in an effort to procure their alliance, or at least neutrality, in the coming war with the British.

On August 25, the two groups smoked the pipe of peace and exchanged the ritual words of diplomatic friendship. Following the ceremonies, the Colonial commissioners told the Iroquois:

Our business with you, besides rekindling the ancient council-fire, and renewing the covenant, and brightening up every link of the chain is, in the first place, to inform you of the advice that was given about thirty years ago, by your wise forefathers, in a great council which was held at Lancaster, in Pennsylvania, when Canassatego spoke to us, the white people, in these very words.

The commissioners then repeated, almost word for word, Canassatego's advice that the colonies form a federal union like that of the Iroquois, as it had appeared in the treaty account published by Franklin's press. The commissioners continued their speech:

> *These were the words of Canassatego. Brothers, Our forefathers rejoiced to hear Canassatego speak these words. They sunk deep into our hearts. The advice was good. It was kind. They said to one another: "The Six Nations are a wise people, Let us hearken to them, and take their counsel, and teach our children to follow it." Our old men have done so. They have frequently taken a single arrow and said, Children, see how easily it is broken. Then they have taken and tied twelve arrows together with a strong string or cord and our strongest men could not break them. See, said they, this is what the Six Nations mean. Divided, a single man may destroy you; united, you are a match for the whole world. We thank the great God that we are all united; that we have a strong confederacy, composed of twelve provinces. . . . These provinces have lighted a great council fire at Philadelphia and sent sixty-five counsellors to speak and act in the name of the whole, and to consult for the common good of the people. . . .*

CHAPTER FIVE

Philosopher as Savage

The Care and Labour of providing for Artificial and Fashionable Wants, the sight of so many rich wallowing in Superfluous plenty, whereby so many are kept poor and distressed for Want, the Insolence of Office . . . and restraints of Custom, all contrive to disgust them [Indians] with what we call civil Society.
> —Benjamin Franklin, marginalia in Matthew Wheelock, Reflections, Moral and Political on Great Britain and Her Colonies, 1770

When the news that the war with France had been won reached Philadelphia, church bells and ceremonial cannon called the people into the streets for the customary celebration. The city, now the second largest in the British Empire with 20,000 people, was entering its golden age as the commercial and political center of the Atlantic Seaboard. Now, history seemed to promise it a role as gem of an entire continent, or at least that small part of it settled by Europeans and their descendants.

Benjamin Franklin, fifty-seven years old and four decades a Philadelphian, was by 1763 unquestionably the city's first citizen. Because of his diplomacy with the Iroquois, which helped procure the victory his compatriots now celebrated, Franklin had gone to

[77]

London to represent the colony at the Royal Court. His wit and wisdom, his talent for diplomacy and municipal organization, his business talents and his scientific achievements—all had earned for Franklin a reputation on both sides of the Atlantic. He was at the peak of an enormously diverse and productive professional life.

Not long after the last bell chime of celebration had died away, however, was there new trouble on the frontier, and new problems for Franklin, who never lost the empathy for the Indians he had acquired first by publishing treaty accounts, then by taking part in treaty councils. Following the eviction of the French, the Iroquois and their allies had lost their leverage as a balance of power. The British now had them surrounded, at least in theory. Hundreds, then thousands, of immigrants, most of them Scotch-Irish, were moving through the passes of the Appalachians, into the Ohio country, taking what seemed to them the just spoils of war. This wasn't, however, French territory. Even by the Crown's law, it still belonged to the Iroquois and their allies. As the illegal migration continued, the covenant chain rusted badly.

British officials, who always kept a hawk's eye on the expense accounts of their Indian agents, cut gift gifting drastically, even for items (such as lead) on which many Indians had grown dependent. Rumors ran through the Indian country that the Great Father across the water was going to kill all the beaver, starve the Indians, and make slaves of them. The younger warriors of many nations became restless, ready to address the problem, even if it cost them their lives. Canassatego, Hendrick, and Weiser, three among many who had maintained the alliance, were dead. In the Grand Council at Onondaga, the sachems argued and the confederacy quivered. In the West, Pontiac fashioned his own alliance and went to war against the squatters.

When the news reached the Pennsylvania frontier that Indians were laying a track of blood through the Ohio Valley, a hunger for revenge arose among the new settlers. They organized vigilante groups and declared virtual secession from the Quaker capital. There the assembly, without an army, was doing all it could in a nonviolent way, to restrain the pellmell rush across the mountains until land could be acquired by treaty. Without loyalty to or even knowledge of the old understandings, the new settlers would neither wait for diplomacy nor be bound by decrees.

On December 14, 1763, fifty-seven vigilantes from Paxton and Donegal, two frontier towns, rode into Conestoga Manor, an Indian settlement, and killed six of twenty Indians living there. Two weeks later, more than 200 "Paxton Men" (as they were now called) invaded Lancaster, where the remaining fourteen Conestoga Indians had been placed in a workhouse for their own protection. Smashing in the workhouse door as the outnumbered local militia looked on, the Paxton Men killed the rest of the Conestoga band, leaving the bodies in a heap within sight of the places where the Anglo-Iroquois alliance had been cemented less than two decades before.

The day before that massacre, Governor William Penn had relayed to the Pennsylvania assembly reports that the Paxton Men's next target would be Philadelphia itself, where they planned to slaughter 140 Indians at Province Island. The governor, citing "attacks on government," asked General Gage to delegate British troops to his Colonial command. Penn also wrote hastily to William Johnson, begging him to break the news of the massacres to the Grand Council at Onondaga "by the properest method."

Franklin responded to the massacres with the most enraged piece of penmanship ever to come off his press—*A Narrative of the Late Massacres in Lancaster County of a Number of Indians, Friends of this Province, by Persons Unknown.* The essay, published in late January 1764, displayed a degree of entirely humorless anger that Franklin rarely used in his writings:

[79   ]

But the Wickedness cannot be Covered, the Guilt will lie on the Whole Land, till Justice is done on the Murderers. THE BLOOD OF THE INNOCENT WILL CRY TO HEAVEN FOR VENGEANCE!

Franklin began his essay by noting that the Conestogas, a dying remnant of the Iroquois confederacy, had been surrounded by frontier settlements, and had dwindled to twenty people, "viz. 7 Men, 5 Women and 8 Children, Boys and Girls, living in Friendship with their White Neighbors, who love them for their peaceable inoffensive Behavior."

Listing most of the victims by name, Franklin wrote that many had adopted the names of "such English persons as they particularly esteem." He provided capsule biographies to show just how inoffensive the Indians had been: "Betty, a harmless old woman and her son, Peter, a likely young Lad."

As Franklin reconstructed the story, the Paxton Men had gathered in the night, surrounding the village at Conestoga Manor, then riding into it at daybreak, "firing upon, stabbing and hatcheting to death" the three men, two women, and one young boy they found. The other fourteen Indians were visiting white neighbors at the time, some to sell brooms and baskets they had made, others to socialize. After killing the six Indians, the vigilantes "scalped and otherwise horribly mangled," them, then burned the village to the ground before riding off in several directions to foil detection.

Two weeks later, when the scene was repeated at the Lancaster workhouse, the Indians, according to Franklin's account, "fell to their Knees, protesting their Love of the English . . . and in this Posture they all received the Hatchet. Men, Women, little Children—were every one inhumanely murdered—in cold Blood!" While some Indians might be "rum debauched and trader corrupted," wrote Franklin, the victims of this massacre were innocent of any crime against the English.

At considerable length, Franklin went on to reflect on the qualities of savagery and civility, using the massacres to illustrate his point: that no race had a monopoly on virtue. To Franklin, the Paxton Men had behaved like "Christian White Savages." He cried out to a just God to punish those who carried the Bible in one hand and the hatchet in the other: "O ye unhappy Perpetrators of this Horrid Wickedness!"

On February 4, a few days after Franklin's broadside hit the streets, the assembly heard more reports that several hundred vigilantes were assembling at Lancaster to march on Philadelphia, and Province Island, to slaughter the Indians encamped there. Governor Penn, recalling Franklin's talent at raising a volunteer militia, hurried to the sage's three-story brick house on Market Street at midnight. Breathlessly climbing the stairs, a retinue of aides in tow, he humbly asked Franklin's help in organizing an armed force to meet the assault from the frontier. To Franklin, the moment was delicious, for eight years before Penn had been instrumental in getting British authorities to order the abolition of Franklin's volunteer militia.

During two days of frenzied activity, Franklin's house became the military headquarters of the province. An impromptu militia of Quakers was raised and armed, and Franklin traveled westward to the frontier with a delegation to face down the frontier insurgents. As Franklin later explained in a letter to Lord Kames, the Scottish philosopher:

> I wrote a pamphlet entitled A Narrative &c (which I think I sent you) to strengthen the hands of our weak Government, by rendering the proceedings of the rioters unpopular and odious. This had a good effect, and afterwards when a great Body of them with Arms march'd towards the Capital in defiance of the Government, with an avowed resolution to put to death 140 Indian converts under its protection, I form'd

an Association at the Governor's request. . . . Near 1,000 of the Citizens accordingly took arms; Governor Penn made my house for some time his Head Quarters, and did everything by my Advice.

While his timely mobilization may have saved the 140 Indians' lives, the sage's actions drained his political capital among whites, especially on the frontier.

Such actions "made myself many enemies among the populace," Franklin wrote. What Franklin called "the whole weight of the proprietary interest" joined against him to "get me out of the Assembly, which was accordingly effected in the last election. . . ." Franklin was sent off to England during early November 1764, "being accompanied to the Ship, 16 miles, by a Cavalcade of three Hundred of my friends, who filled our sails with their good Wishes." A month later, Franklin began work as Pennsylvania's agent to the Crown.

The rest of the decade was a time of instability on the frontier. Franklin was in frequent correspondence with his son, William Franklin, and with William Johnson, who kept the elder Franklin posted on problems they encountered with squatters. Johnson wrote to Franklin July 10, 1766: "I daily dread a Rupture with the Indians occasioned by the Licentious Conduct of the frontier Inhabitants who continue to Rob and Murder them." William wrote to his father three days later: "There have been lately several Murders of Indians in the different Provinces. Those committed in this Province will be duly enquired into, and the Murderers executed, as soon as found guilty. They are all apprehended and secured in Gaol."

For the rest of his life, shuttling between America, England, and France on various diplomatic assignments, Franklin continued to develop his philosophy with abundant references to the Indian societies he had observed so closely during his days as envoy to the Six Nations. Franklin's combination of indigenous American thought and European heritage earned him the title among his contemporaries as America's first philosopher. In Europe, he was sometimes called "the philosopher as savage."*

"Franklin could not help but admire the proud, simple life of America's native inhabitants," wrote Conner in *Poor Richard's Politicks* (1965). "There was a noble quality in the stories . . . which he told of their hospitality and tolerance, of their oratory and pride." Franklin, said Conner, saw in Indians' conduct "a living symbol of simplicity and 'happy mediocrity . . .' exemplifying essential aspects of the Virtuous Order." Depiction of this "healthful, primitive morality could be instructive for transplanted Englishmen, still doting on 'foreign Geegaws'; 'happiness,' Franklin wrote, 'is more generally and equally diffused among savages than in our civilized societies.' "

"Happy mediocrity" meant striking a compromise between the overcivilization of Europe, with its distinctions between rich and poor and consequent corruption, and the egalitarian, democratic societies of the Indians that formed a counterpoint to European monarchy. The Virtuous Order would combine both, borrowing from Europe arts, sciences, and mechanical skills, taking from the Indians aspects of the natural society that Franklin and others believed to be a window on the pasts of other cultures, including those from which the colonists had come. There is in the writings of Franklin, as well as those of Jefferson, a sense of using the Indian example to recapture natural rights that Europeans had lost under monarchy. The European experience was not to be reconstructed on American soil. Instead, Franklin (as well as Jefferson) sought to erect an amalgam, a combination of indigenous American Indian practices and the cultural heritage that the new

---

* See: Peter Gay, "Enlightenment Thought and the American Revolution," in John R. Howe, Jr., ed., *The Role of Ideology in the American Revolution* (New York: Holt, Rinehart and Winston, 1970), p. 48.

Americans had carried from Europe. In discussing the new culture, Franklin and others drew from experience with native Americans, which was more extensive than that of the European natural rights philosophers. The American Indians' theory and practice affected Franklin's observations on the need for appreciation of diverse cultures and religions, public opinion as the basis for a polity, the nature of liberty and happiness, and the social role of property. American Indians also appear frequently in some of Franklin's scientific writings. At a time much less specialized than the twentieth century, Franklin and his associates (such as Colden and Jefferson) did not think it odd to cross from philosophy to natural science to practical politics.

Franklin's writings on American Indians were remarkably free of ethnocentricism, although he often used words such as "savages," which carry more prejudicial connotations in the twentieth century than in his time. Franklin's cultural relativism was perhaps one of the purest expressions of Enlightenment assumptions that stressed racial equality and the universality of moral sense among peoples. Systematic racism was not called into service until a rapidly expanding frontier demanded that enemies be dehumanized during the rapid, historically inevitable westward movement of the nineteenth century. Franklin's respect for cultural diversity did not reappear widely as an assumption in Euro-American thought until Franz Boas and others revived it around the end of the nineteenth century. Franklin's writings on Indians express the fascination of the Enlightenment with nature, the natural origins of man and society, and natural (or human) rights. They are likewise imbued with a search (which amounted at times almost to a ransacking of the past) for alternatives to monarchy as a form of government, and to orthodox state-recognized churches as a form of worship.

Franklin's sense of cultural relativism often led him to see events from an Indian perspective, as when he advocated Colonial union and regulation of the Indian trade at the behest of the Iroquois. His relativism was expressed clearly in the opening lines of an essay, "Remarks Concerning the Savages of North America," which may have been written as early as the 1750s (following Franklin's first extensive personal contact with Indians) but was not published until 1784.

> *Savages we call them, because their manners differ from ours, which we think the Perfection of Civility; they think the same of theirs. . . . Perhaps, if we could examine the Manners of different Nations with Impartiality, we should find no People so rude, as to be without any Rules of Politeness; nor any so polite, as not to have some Remains of Rudeness.*

In this essay, Franklin also observed that "education" must be measured against cultural practices and needs:

> *Having few artificial Wants, they [Indians] have abundance of Leisure for Improvement by Conversation. Our laborious Manner of Life, compared with theirs, they esteem slavish and base; and the Learning, on which we value ourselves, they regard as frivolous and useless.*

Franklin illustrated this point by recounting an exchange between the commissioners of Virginia and the Iroquois at the 1744 Lancaster treaty council. The account of the treaty, written by Conrad Weiser, reported that the Virginia commissioners asked the Iroquois to send a few of their young men to a college in Williamsburg (probably William and Mary) where "they would be well provided for, and instructed in the Learning of the White People." The Iroquois took the matter under advisement for a day (to be polite, Franklin indicated) and answered the Virginia commissioners July 4, the same day that Canassatego advised the colonists to form a union. Canassatego answered for the Iroquois a few minutes after his advice regarding the union:

> *We must let you know that we love our Children too well to send them so great a Way, and the Indians are not inclined to give their Children Learning. We allow it to be good, and thank you for your Invitation; but our customs differing from yours, you will be so good as to excuse us.*

Franklin's essay was taken almost exactly from the 1744 treaty account published by his Philadelphia press during that year; in the essay, Franklin related that Canassatego told the commissioners that his people had had experience with such proposals before. "Several of our young people were formerly brought up at the Colleges of the Northern Provinces," the sachem said. "They were instructed in all your Sciences, but when they came back to us, they were bad Runners, ignorant of every means of living in the Woods, unable to bear either cold or hunger. . . ." The young men educated in Euro-American schools were "good for nothing," Canassatego asserted. In Franklin's account, Canassatego not only turned down the commissioner's offer with polite firmness, but made a counter-offer himself: "If the Gentlemen of Virginia will send us a Dozen of their Sons, we will take great care of their Education, instruct them in all we know, and make *Men* of them."

Franklin's "Remarks Concerning the Savages" shows an appreciation of the Indian councils, which he had written were superior in some ways to the British Parliament. "Having frequent Occasion to hold public Councils, they have acquired great Order and Decency in conducting them. . . . The women . . . are the Records of the Council . . . who take exact notice of what passes and imprint it in their Memories, to communicate it to their Children."

Franklin also showed appreciation of the sharpness of memory fostered by reliance on oral communication: "They preserve traditions of Stipulations in Treaties 100 Years back; which, when we compare with our writings, we always find exact." When a speaker at an Indian council (the reference was probably to the Iroquois) had completed his remarks, he was given a few minutes to recollect his thoughts, and to add anything that might have been forgotten. "To interrupt another, even in common Conversation, is reckon'd highly indecent. How different this is to the conduct of a polite British House of Commons, where scarce a day passes without some Confusion, that makes the Speaker hoarse in calling *to Order*." Indian customs in conversation were reflected in *Poor Richard* for 1753, the year of Franklin's first diplomatic assignment, to negotiate the Carlisle Treaty: "A pair of good Ears will drain dry a Thousand Tongues." Franklin also compared this Indian custom favorably with "the Mode of Conversation of many polite Companies of Europe, where, if you do not deliver your Sentence with great Rapidity, you are cut off in the middle of it by the impatient Loquacity of those you converse with, and never suffer'd to finish it!" Some white missionaries had been confused by Indians who listened to their sermons patiently, and then refused to believe them, Franklin wrote.

To Franklin, the order and decorum of Indian councils were important to them because their government relied on public opinion: "All their Government is by Counsel of the Sages; there is no Force, there are no Prisons, no officers to compel Obedience, or inflict Punishment." Indian leaders study oratory, and the best speaker had the most influence, Franklin observed. In words that would be echoed by Jefferson, Franklin used the Indian model as an exemplar of government with a minimum of governance. This sort of democracy was governed not by fiat, but by public opinion and consensus-creating custom:

[87]

*All of the Indians of North America not under the domin-
ion of the Spaniards are in that natural state, being re-
strained by no laws, having no Courts, or Ministers of Justice, no Suits, no Prisons, no Governors vested with any
Legal Authority. The Persuasion of Men distinguished by
Reputation of Wisdom is the only means by which others
are govern'd or rather led—and the State of the Indians was
probably the first State of all Nations.*

Franklin also compared the Indians' offers of free lodging and
food for visitors to the customs of Euro-Americans. The Iroquois
kept guest houses for travelers. This custom was contrasted by
Franklin with Indians' treatment in white towns. He recounted a
conversation between Conrad Weiser and Canassatego, who were
close friends. In that conversation, Canassatego said to Weiser:

*If a white Man, in travelling thro' our country, enters one of
our cabins, we treat him as I treat you; we dry him if he is
wet, we warm him if he is cold, we give him Meat and
Drink that he may allay his Thirst and Hunger; and we
spread soft furs for him to rest and sleep on; we demand
nothing in return. But, if I go to a white man's house in Albany, and ask for Victuals and Drink, they say "Where is
your Money?" And if I have none, they say, "Get out, you
Indian Dog!"*

Franklin was also given to affecting Indian speech patterns in
some of his writings, another indication that his respect for diverse cultures enhanced his understanding of the Indians with
whom he often associated. In 1787, he described the American
political system in distinctly Iroquoian terms to an unnamed Indian correspondent:

*I am sorry that the Great Council Fire of our Nation is not
now burning, so that you cannot do your business there. In*

a few months, the coals will be rak'd out of the ashes and will again be kindled. Our wise men will then take the complaints . . . of your Nation into consideration and take the proper Measures for giving you Satisfaction.

Franklin was also fond of calling on the Great Spirit when he could do so in appreciative company.

Religious self-righteousness and pomposity was a favorite target of Franklin's pen, and he often used Indians to illustrate the religious relativism that was basic to his own Deistic faith. Deism, a religion that more than any other was prototypical of the Enlightenment frame of mind, emphasized naturalism, natural man, and rational inquiry, all of which finely complemented Franklin's interests in Indian cultures. Like Colden before him and Jefferson after him, Franklin often used his Deist beliefs to stress the universality of moral sense among peoples, and to break down ethnocentricity. Many of the people who were closest to the Indians during this period were Deists; calling on the Great Spirit was not at all out of character for them.

According to Alfred O. Aldridge *(Benjamin Franklin and Nature's God,* 1967), Deism involved belief in the superiority of "natural religion" as opposed to "the hollow formalism of Christianity." Deism formed an ideal complement to the natural rights philosophy that was so important in Enlightenment thought. According to Aldridge, Franklin's early *Articles of Belief* (1728) showed that, early in his life, many of his religious beliefs resembled those of several American Indians. At that time, Franklin even accepted polytheism. Although he later acknowledged monotheism, Franklin never lost his critical eye toward conventional Christianity. Aldridge found in Franklin's "Remarks Concerning the Savages of North America" an abundant satire of religious proselytizing and economic imperialism.

In his "Remarks Concerning the Savages . . ." Franklin described a Swedish minister who lectured a group of Susquehanah

Indians on the story of the creation, including "the Fall of our first parents from eating an Apple, the coming of Christ to repair the Mischief, his Miracles and Suffering &c." The Indians replied that it was, indeed, bad to eat apples, when they could have been made into cider. They then repaid the missionary's storytelling favor by telling him their own creation story. The missionary was aghast at this comparison of Christianity with what he regarded as heathenism and, according to Franklin, replied: "What I delivered to you are Sacred Truths, but what you tell me is mere Fable, Fiction and Falsehood." The Indians, in turn, told the missionary that he was lacking in manners:

> My brother [the Indians told the missionary], it seems that your friends have not done you Justice in your Education, that they have not well instructed you in the Rules of Common Civility. You saw that we, who understand and practise those Rules, believ'd all your stories. Why do you refuse to believe ours?

In the same essay, Franklin commented on the use of religion as a cover for economic exploitation. Again he used Canassatego, in conversations related to Franklin by Weiser. According to Franklin, Canassatego asked Weiser: "Conrad, you have lived long among the white People, and know something of their Customs. I have sometimes been to Albany and noticed that once in Seven Days they shut up their shops and assemble in the Great House; tell me: what is it for?"

Weiser was said by Franklin to have replied: "They meet there to learn *Good Things*."

Canassatego had no doubt that the town merchants were hearing "good things" in the church, but he doubted that all those good things were purely religious. He had recently visited Albany to trade beaver pelts for blankets, knives, powder, rum, and other things. He asked a merchant, Hans Hanson, about trading, and

Hanson told the sachem that he couldn't talk business because it was time for the meeting to hear good things in the great house. After the merchants returned from the church, Canassatego found that all of them had fixed the price of beaver at three shillings sixpence a pound. "This made it clear to me, that my suspicion was right; and that whatever they pretended of meeting to learn Good Things, the real purpose was to consult how to cheat Indians in the Price of Beaver," the sachem said, according to Franklin's account.

In *Poor Richard* for 1751, Franklin wrote: "To Christians bad rude Indians we prefer/ 'Tis better not to know than knowing err." Unlike Franklin, many English Deists had never seen an Indian, but they, too, often assumed that "the American natives would have a religion akin to Deism—one based on the commonly observed phenomena of nature and dedicated to the worship of Nature's God," Aldridge wrote. Franklin saw the similarity of his own faith to that of Indians confirmed through personal experience. Deists, like Franklin, who sought to return "to the simplicity of nature" appeared to see things worth emulating in Indian societies.

Franklin's use of Canassatego, to twit conventional Christianity, was not unique in his time. Satirists on both sides of the Atlantic used the testaments of real or fictitious Indians to deflate the righteousness of clerics; did the Indians not have their own theories of the earth's origin?

Canassatego also figured importantly in an elaborate hoax intended to ridicule conventional Christianity, which appeared in the *London Chronicle* in June 1768. The hoax involved a review of a nonexistent book, *The Captivity of William Henry*. The fake review was not signed, so it is not possible to prove that Franklin wrote it. Whoever did concoct the hoax knew quite a bit about Iroquois society and customs, which made Franklin an obvious candidate. The style of the hoax fits Franklin, but some rather obvious errors point away from Franklin's authorship. For example, William Henry was purportedly taken captive in 1755 when he met Canassatego, who, in point of fact, had died in 1750. Regardless of its authorship, the hoax illustrated the use that was made of Indians as a counterpoint to conventional Christianity at the time. Such publications tended to legitimatize religious pluralism.

As they sought a middle ground between the corrupting over-civilization of Europe and the simplicity of the state of nature in which they believed that many Indians lived, Franklin and other Deists paid abundant attention to the political organization of the Indians, especially the Iroquois, who were not only the best organized Indian polity with which British Americans had contact, but who were also allied with them. "Franklin had the conception of an original, pre-political state of nature in which men were absolutely free and equal—a condition he thought admirably illustrated among the American Indians," Eiselen wrote in *Franklin's Political Theories* (1928). Franklin himself wrote: "Their wants . . . [are] supplied by the spontaneous Productions of Nature" and that they did not at all want to be "civilized."

This state of nature was eagerly sought by many eighteenth-century Euro-Americans. To understand how many Europeans left their own cultures to live with the Indians is to realize just how permeable the frontier was. To those who remained behind, it was often rumored that those who had gone over to the Indians had been "captured." While some captives were taken, more often the whites took up Indian life without compulsion. As Franklin wrote to Peter Collinson May 9, 1753:

The proneness of human Nature to a life of ease, of freedom from care and labour appears strongly in the heretofore little success that has attended every attempt to civilize our American Indians. . . . They visit us frequently and see the advantages that Arts, Science and compact Society procure us; they are not deficient in natural understanding and yet they have never shewn any inclination to change their manner of life for ours, or to learn any of our Arts.

While Indians did not seem to have much inclination to exchange their culture for the Euro-American, many Euro-Americans appeared more than willing to become Indians at this time:

When an Indian child has been brought up among us, taught our language and habituated to our customs, yet if he goes to see his relations and makes one Indian Ramble with them, there is no perswading him ever to return. And that this is not natural [only to Indians], but as men, is plain from this, that when white persons of either sex have been taken prisoners young by the Indians, and lived awhile among them, tho' ransomed by their Friends, and treated with all imaginable tenderness to prevail with them to stay among the English, yet within a Short time they become disgusted with our manner of Life, and the care and pains that are necessary to support it, and take the first good Opportunity of escaping again into the Woods, from whence there is no reclaiming them.

Franklin followed with an example. He had heard of a person who had been "reclaimed" from the Indians and returned to a sizable estate. Tired of the care needed to maintain such a style of life, he had turned it over to his younger brother and, taking only a rifle and a matchcoat, "took his way again to the Wilderness." Franklin used this story to illustrate his point that "No European who has tasted Savage Life can afterwards bear to live in our societies." Such societies, wrote Franklin, provided their members with greater opportunities for happiness than European cultures. Continuing, he said:

The Care and Labour of providing for Artificial and fashionable Wants, the sight of so many Rich wallowing in superfluous plenty, whereby so many are kept poor and distress'd for Want, the Insolence of Office . . . the restraints of Custom, all contrive to disgust them with what we call civil Society.

With so many white people willingly becoming associated with Indian societies, it was not difficult for thoughts and customs practiced behind the frontier to leak back into the colonies.

Franklin's interest in America's indigenous peoples was not restricted to their social and political systems. Like many European and American scientists of his time, Franklin was interested in tracing the origins of these "natural men" who figure so importantly in the thought of the Enlightenment. Since they were believed to be living in a state that approximated the origins of all peoples, Indians made fascinating objects of scientific study. Franklin, an anthropologist before the discipline had a name, engaged in the collection of Indian grammars, an activity practiced on both sides of the Atlantic during the eighteenth century. By the end of the century, missionaries, natural scientists, and others had produced dozens of grammars in many Indian languages of varying length and accuracy, one indication of the Enlightenment era's intense fascination with the peoples of the New World. Thomas Jefferson, George Washington, and others collected the grammars and searched for words that might resemble concepts or phrases in English, French, German, Welsh, Yiddish, or other European languages. Many popular theories supposed that various Indian tribes might have descended from the Welsh, or the Jews, or the Celts, and linguistic ties were believed to support those theories.

As a scientist Franklin also vigorously opposed degeneracy theories, an intellectual export from Europe. These theories were

developed to their highest form in France as a reaction to the
myth of the "Noble Savage," which flourished in the same nation
at the same time. According to the theory of degeneracy, America's climate degraded all life forms that existed there. Plants,
animals, Indians, and transplanted Europeans were all said to be
subject to this debilitating influence. Franklin thought otherwise.
In 1772, he replied to assertions by de Pauw and Count de Buffon, writing to an unnamed French friend: *"Les Américains ne le
cédent ni en force, ni en courage, ni en d'esprit aux Européens."*
Franklin had too much personal contact to accept either the conception of the Noble Savage or the degeneracy argument. Unlike
the Europeans who argued over land and people most of them
had never seen, Franklin knew both well, and this knowledge produced in his writings about America and American Indians a
pragmatism that many Europeans lacked.

"The savage," wrote de Buffon, "is feeble and has small organs
of generation. He has neither hair nor beard, and no ardor whatever for his female." To de Buffon, Indians were also "less sensitive, and yet more timid and cowardly . . . [with] no activity of
mind." If not forced to move in order to survive, Indians "will rest
stupidly . . . lying down for several days." Indians, wrote de Buffon, "look upon their wives . . . only as beasts of burden." The
men, in de Buffon's analysis, lacked sexual capacity: "Nature, by
refusing him the power of love, has treated him worse and lowered
him deeper than any animal."

To Jefferson, de Buffon—who had never seen America, nor the
Indians he wrote about—presented a fat and inviting target. Jefferson replied that no correlation existed between sexual ardor and
the amount of body hair on a man. "With them it is disgraceful to
be hairy on the body. They say it likens them to hogs. They
therefore pluck the hair as fast as it appears," Jefferson wrote. He
recounted Indians' bravery in war to refute de Buffon's assertion

that they were timid and cowardly, and he cited examples of Indian oratory to show that America's natives were not mentally deficient. While Jefferson believed that Indians' sexual equipment and drive was not less than that of whites, he wondered whether constant hunting and the Indians' diet might have diminished those natural gifts. What raised such a question in his mind, Jefferson did not say.

As with many scientific debates through the ages, the emotional exchanges between Europeans and Americans over the degeneracy theories reflected the political and social conflicts of the age. In the writings of Franklin there seems to be an emerging awareness of a distinctive American habit of mind, a sense that these transplanted Europeans, himself included, were becoming something not inferior to Europeans, but something very different. As the debate over degeneracy theories was taking place, more and more Americans were, like Franklin, coming to conclude that history and dignity demanded the colonies become a separate nation. Franklin more than once rushed to the defense of America and things American. When British publishers derided American cuisine, he hurried into print with a defense of American (Indian) corn, replete with recipes. When French authors peddled fantasies about the wildness of America and the savagery of its native inhabitants, Franklin set up a press in Passy and issued from it essays on the virtues of America and Americans, white and red.

During the decade after the Stamp Act, Franklin's writings developed into an argument for American distinctiveness, a sense of nationhood in a new land, a sense that an entirely new age was dawning for the Americans who traced their roots to Europe. The new nation would not be European, but American—combining both heritages to make a specifically different culture. Franklin and his contemporaries, among whom one of the most articulate was Jefferson, were setting out to invent a nation. Before they could have a nation, however, they had to break with Britain, an act that called for an intellectual backdrop for rebellion, and a rationale for revolution.

CHAPTER SIX

Self-Evident Truths

I am convinced that those societies [as the Indians] which live without government enjoy in their general mass an infinitely greater degree of happiness than those who live under European governments.

—Thomas Jefferson to Edward Carrington, 1787

Philadelphia became the intellectual nerve center of revolution in the mid-1770s. The Continental Congress convened there. The Declaration of Independence was drafted there, and first posted there, six weeks before the news reached the royal court in London at which it was directed. Philadelphia, the new capital of the new confederacy—its "Grand Council fire," as Franklin called the city in some of his letters—was becoming the commercial center of Eastern North America. The city's stately public buildings gave it an air of a capital beyond its years. When the Declaration of Independence was first posted along its streets, the Quaker city was not even a century old. Barely ninety years after the Penn family's surveyors had first marked it out of the wilderness, Philadelphia was surrounded by the mansions of merchants who had helped make it the busiest port on the Atlantic Seaboard, as well

[98]

as the political and intellectual center of the colonies. The mansions reclined in baronial style along the rivers that converged at the commercial center, looking a little like English estates. Beyond these patches of tamed greenery, Philadelphians looked westward into the maw of a continent of immense size, which was to their eyes at once wild, dark, and threatening, as well as a possible source of riches beyond imagination. Rather suddenly, the men and women who had peopled a few widely scattered English colonies and stitched them together were faced with the task of making a nation, in area larger by far than any in Western Europe.

Franklin had always lived in the city's center, and never moved to the outskirts, even when his finances allowed. During the debates that welded the colonies into a nation he remained in the three-story brick house on Market Street that he had designed with his wife, Deborah, before the conclusion of the war with France. When the weather was fair, he could walk to Independence Hall. A year after skirmishes at Lexington and Concord turned angry words into armed rebellion, when the delegates to the Continental Congress decided that a rationale for the revolution needed to be put on paper, Franklin was the most likely candidate to write the manifesto. He had just returned from a long and difficult trip to the Ohio country, and had come down with gout. His three score and ten years showing on him, Franklin declined invitations to write the Declaration of Independence. He did join the drafting committee, and eventually became Thomas Jefferson's major editor.

At the age of thirty-three, however, Jefferson was not at all sure that he was equal to the task of telling the world why the colonies were breaking with Britain. On June 11, 1776, when he was asked by the Continental Congress to serve on a committee that would draft the declaration, Jefferson asked to be excused from the congress so that he could return to Williamsburg where he planned to help write the Virginia Constitution. His request for a leave denied, Jefferson asked John Adams, another member of the drafting committee, to write the document. Adams refused.

"Why will you not?" Jefferson asked Adams. "You ought to do it."

"Reasons enough," said Adams.

"What are your reasons?"

"First," said Adams, "you are a Virginian, and a Virginian ought to appear at the head of this business. Second: I am obnoxious, suspected and unpopular. You are very much otherwise. Third: You can write ten times better than I can."

"Well," replied Jefferson, "If you are decided, I will do as well as I can."

Adams respected Jefferson's "masterly pen." The young man from Virginia brought with him to the Continental Congress what Adams called "a reputation for literature, science and a happy talent for composition. Writings of his "were remarkable for . . . peculiar felicity of expression," in Adams's opinion. Like many talented writers, Jefferson did not like to compose for committees. He called changes made in his drafts by other delegates to the Continental Congress "depredations."

While he didn't always welcome changes in his prose, Jefferson easily accepted criticism and corrections from Franklin, who by this time was regarded as an elder statesman in Europe as well as in America. Franklin himself had learned, from long experience, the trials attending composition of "papers to be reviewed by a public body." Jefferson, who was learning the same, willingly submitted his drafts to Franklin and Adams.

Between 1775 and 1791, when Franklin died, his political life overlapped Jefferson's. He venerated the elderly sage, and expressed his admiration frequently. Following Franklin at the post of United States ambassador to France, Jefferson was often asked:

"Is it you, Sir, who replace Dr. Franklin?" Jefferson would reply: "No one can replace him, Sir, I am just his successor."

"There appeared to me to be more respect and veneration attached to the character of Doctor Franklin than to any other person in the same country, foreign or native. . . . When he left Passy, it seemed as if the village had lost its patriarch," Jefferson recalled. Having admired Franklin so, it was not surprising that where Franklin laid down an intellectual thread, Jefferson often picked it up. Jefferson's writings clearly show that he shared Franklin's respect for Indian thought. Both men represented the Enlightenment frame of mind of which the American Indians seemed a practical example. Both knew firsthand the Indian way of life. Both shared with the Indian the wild, rich land out of which the Indian had grown. It was impossible that that experience should not have become woven into the debates and philosophical musings that gave the nation's founding instruments their distinctive character. In so far as the nation still bears these marks of its birth, we are all "Indians"—if not in our blood, then in the thinking that to this day shapes many of our political and social assumptions. Jefferson's declaration expressed many of these ideas:

> We hold these truths to be self–evident, that all men are created equal, that they are endowed by their Creator with certain inalienable rights, that among these are Life, Liberty and the Pursuit of Happiness. That, to secure these rights, Governments are instituted among Men, deriving their just powers from the consent of the governed. That, when any form of government becomes destructive of these ends, it is the Right of the People to alter or abolish it.

The newly united colonies had assumed "among the Powers of the earth, the separate and equal station to which the Laws of Nature and Nature's God entitle them," Jefferson wrote. The declaration was being made, he said, because "a decent respect for the opinions of mankind requires that they should declare the causes which impel them to the separation."

There were few ideas in the declaration (outside of the long list of wrongs committed by the Crown) that did not owe more than a little to Franklin's and Jefferson's views of American Indian societies. In drawing sanction for independence from the laws of nature, Jefferson was also drawing from the peoples beyond the frontiers of the new nation who lived in what late eighteenth-century Enlightenment thinkers believed to be a state of nature. The "pursuit of happiness" and the "consent of the governed" were exemplified in Indian polities to which Jefferson (like Franklin) often referred in his writings. The Indian in Jefferson's mind (as in Franklin's) served as a metaphor for liberty.

Jefferson wrote to Edward Carrington January 16, 1787:

> The way to prevent these irregular interpositions of the people is to give them full information of their affairs thro' the public papers, and to contrive that those papers should penetrate the whole mass of the people. The basis of our government being the opinion of the people, our very first object should be to keep that right; and were it left to me to decide whether we should have a government without newspapers or newspapers without a government, I should not hesitate a moment to prefer the latter. . . . I am convinced that those societies [as the Indians] which live without government enjoy in their general mass an infinitely greater degree of happiness than those who live under European governments.

Echoing Franklin's earlier comment, Jefferson looked across the frontier and found societies where social cohesion was provided by consensus instead of by the governmental apparatus used to maintain control in Europe. Among the Indians, wrote Jefferson, "Public opinion is in the place of law, and restrains morals as powerfully as laws ever did anywhere." The contrast to Europe was obvious: "Under pretence of governing, they have divided their nations into two classes, wolves and sheep. I do not exaggerate. This is a true picture of Europe." Returning to America, Jefferson concluded: "Cherish therefore the spirit of our people, and keep alive their attention." To Jefferson, public opinion among the Indians was an important reason for their lack of oppressive government, as well as the egalitarian distribution of property on which Franklin had earlier remarked. Jefferson believed that without the people looking over the shoulder of their leaders, "You and I, the Congress, judges and governors shall all become wolves." The "general prey of the rich on the poor" could be prevented by a vigilant public.

Jefferson believed that freedom to exercise restraint on their leaders, and an egalitarian distribution of property secured for Indians in general a greater degree of happiness than that to be found among the superintended sheep at the bottom of European class structures. Jefferson thought a great deal of "happiness," a word which in the eighteenth century carried connotations of a sense of personal and societal security and well-being that it has since lost. Jefferson thought enough of happiness to make its pursuit a natural right, along with life and liberty. In so doing, he dropped "property," the third member of the natural rights trilogy generally used by followers of John Locke.

Jefferson's writings made it evident that he, like Franklin, saw accumulation of property beyond that needed to satisfy one's natural requirements as an impediment to liberty. To place "property" in the same trilogy with life and liberty, against the backdrop of Jefferson's views regarding the social nature of property, would have been a contradiction, Jefferson composed some of his most trenchant rhetoric in opposition to the erection of a European-like aristocracy on American soil. To Jefferson, the pursuit of happiness appears to have involved neither the accumulation of property beyond basic need, nor the sheer pursuit of mirth. It meant freedom from tyranny, and from want, things not much in abundance in the Europe from which many of Jefferson's countrymen had so recently fled. Jefferson's writings often characterized Europe as a place from which to escape—a corrupt place, where wolves consumed sheep regularly, and any uncalled for bleating by the sheep was answered with a firm blow to the head.

Using the example of the man who left his estate to return to the simplicity of nature, carrying only his rifle and matchcoat with him, Franklin indicated that the accumulation of property brought perils as well as benefits. Franklin argued that the state's power should not be used to skew the distribution of wealth, using Indian society, where "hunting is free for all," as an examplar:

> *Private property . . . is a Creature of Society, and is subject to the Calls of that Society, whenever its Necessities shall require it, even to its last Farthing, its contributors therefore to the public Exingencies are not to be considered a Benefit on the Public, entitling the Contributors to the Distinctions of Honor and Power, but as the Return of an Obligation previously received, or as payment for a just Debt.*

"The important ends of Civil Society, and the personal Securities of Life and Liberty, these remain the same in every Member of the Society," Franklin continued. He concluded: "The poorest continues to have an equal Claim to them with the most opulent, whatever Difference Time, Chance or Industry may occasion in their Circumstances."

Franklin used examples from Indian societies rather explicitly to illustrate his conception of property and its role in society:

> *All property, indeed, except the savage's temporary cabin, his bow, his matchcoat and other little Acquisitions abso-*

lutely necessary for his Subsistence, seems to me to be the creature of public Convention. Hence, the public has the rights of regulating Descents, and all other Conveyances of Property, and even of limiting the quantity and uses of it. All the property that is necessary to a man is his natural Right, which none may justly deprive him of, but all Property superfluous to such Purposes is the property of the Public who, by their Laws have created it and who may, by other Laws dispose of it.

Franklin, a believer in simplicity and "happy mediocrity," thought that an overabundance of possessions inhibited freedom because social regulation was required to keep track of what belonged to whom, and to keep greed from developing into antisocial conflict. He also opposed the use of public office for private profit. If officials were to serve the people rather than exploit them, they should not be compensated for their public service, Franklin stated during debate on the Constitution. "It may be imagined by some that this is a Utopian idea, and that we can never find Men to serve in the Executive Department without paying them well for their Services. I conceive this to be a mistake," Franklin said. On August 10, 1787, also during debate on the Constitution, Franklin opposed property qualifications for election to Congress. So fervent was his opposition to the use of public office for private gain that Franklin wrote in a codacil to his will, "In a democratical state there ought to be no offices of profit."

As well as using Indians as exemplars of their concepts of property, Franklin and other Colonial leaders usually held a rather high intellectual regard for the Indians' own property rights. Without adequate military force, however, they were unable to check the continuing movement of Euro-Americans onto land that had not been ceded by the various Indian nations. In his *Administration of the Colonies*, a text widely used for instruction of Colonial officials during the mid–eighteenth century, Thomas Pownall argued that neither the Pope, nor any other European sovereign, had a right to give away Indian land without their consent.

"The lands [of America] did not belong to the Crown, but to the Indians, of whom the Colonists either purchased them at their own Expence, or conquered them without Assistance from Britain," Franklin wrote in the margin of an anonymous pamphlet, "The True Constitutional Means for Putting an End to the Disputes Between London and the American Colonies," published in London during 1769. Franklin was replying to an assertion in the brochure that the colonists occupied America "by the bounty of the Crown." A year later, Franklin made a similar point, writing in the margin of Wheelock's *Reflections, Moral and Political, on Great Britain and Her Colonies*: "The British Nation has no original Property in the Country of America. It was purchas'd by the first Colonists of the Natives, the only Owners. The Colonies [are] not *created* by Britain, but by the colonists themselves."

By supporting the Indians' claim of original title, Franklin and other advocates of independence undercut Britian's claim to the colonies. A popular argument at the time was that if Britian had a right to assert a claim to America under European law because English people settled there, then Germany had a right to claim England because the Angles and Saxons, Germanic peoples, colonized the British territory. To Franklin, the colonies belonged to the colonists, and what the colonists had not bought from the Indians (or, in some cases, seized in war) belonged to the native peoples.*

---

* While Franklin used Indians' concepts of property to illustrate his own, and while he frequently supported Indians' rights against those of illegal squatters, Franklin was also involved in the land business. In Franklin's mind, it was the illegal taking of land that was objectionable. Legal usurpation, by treaty or even sometimes by military conquest, did not offend his sense of justice. In 1754, the same year that Franklin lob-

In Franklin's mind, there appeared to be no contradiction between orderly expansion of settlement and support of Indian needs for a homeland and sustenance. Looking westward into what he believed to be a boundless forest, Franklin assumed that the Indians would always have land enough to live as they wished. He thought that the continent was so vast that Europeans would not settle the breadth of it for a thousand years. Although both were scientists, technological innovators and politicians, neither Franklin nor Jefferson saw the technological changes or the increase in European immigration that would sweep across the continent in less than a century.

While he didn't forsee the speed of expansion, Franklin was troubled by the greed that he did see emerging in America, a huge and rich table laden with riches, seemingly for the taking. "A rich rogue is like a fat hog, who never does good 'til he's dead as a log,'' he wrote in *Poor Richard* for 1733. In the same edition, he also

---

bied the Iroquois' cause by advocating a union of the colonies, he also drew up a plan for settling the Ohio country, which was at that time occupied by Indian allies of the Iroquois (Labaree and Willcox, *Franklin Papers*, 5:456). Peace between the English and the Iroquois was good for more than alliance against the French; it also made land speculation easier and much less dangerous, as long as the land was acquired with some form of payment and Indian consent. In 1768, Sir William Johnson, Franklin's son William and other Colonial officials who had close ties to the Iroquois, such as George Croghan, worked intensively for Anglo-Iroquois amity at the Fort Stanwix treaty conference. All of them were negotiating large land purchases. Franklin at the time was lobbying for the purchases in England, where he worked as a Colonial agent with the Crown (*Ibid.*, 10:38–39; James Sullivan, *et al.*, *The Papers of Sir William Johnson*, 14 vols. (Albany: University of the State of New York, 1921–1965), 6:129). According to Clarence W. Alvord, Indian war threats were sometimes invented or blown out of proportion during this period in order to get the Crown's attention directed toward peacekeeping, which would make land purchases easier (Alvord, *The Mississippi Valley in British Politics* (Cleveland: Arthur H. Clark Co., 1917), pp. 345–358). Franklin was involved in other land business as well, especially plans to settle the Ohio country (Labaree and Willcox, *Franklin Papers*, 17:135–136).

wrote: "The poor have little, beggars none; the rich too much, enough, not one."

Like Franklin, Jefferson defined property not as a natural right, but as a civil right, bestowed by society and removable by it. To Jefferson and Franklin natural rights were endowed (as the declaration put it) by the Creator, not by kings or queens or legislators or governors. Civil rights were decreed or legislated. As Jefferson wrote to William Short, property is a creature of society:

> While it is a moot question whether the origin of any kind of property is derived from Nature at all . . . it is considered by those who have seriously considered the subject, that no one has, of natural right, a separate property in an acre of land . . . [which] . . . is the property for the moment of him who occupies it, but when he relinquishes that occupation, the property goes with it. Stable ownership is the gift of social law, and is given late in the progress of society.

Societies that gave undue emphasis to protection of property could infringe on the peoples' rights of life, liberty, and happiness. According to Jefferson: "Whenever there is, in any country, uncultivated lands and unemployed poor, it is clear that the laws of property have been so extended as to violate natural right." At the opposite end of Jefferson's intellectual spectrum stood the Indian societies of eastern North America that, in spite of minimal government that impressed Jefferson, had different laws or customs encouraging the accumulation of material wealth. Jefferson, although he retained a vague admiration for this form of "primitive communism" until late in his life, acknowledged that such a structure could not be laid atop a European, or a European-descended, society: "Indian society may be best, but it is not possible for large numbers of people."

While some aspects of Indian society were admirable but impractical, Jefferson found many aspects of European cultures deplorable but likely to be emulated in America if the people and their leaders did not take care to resist them. Jefferson acknowledged late in his life that "a right of property is founded in our natural wants," but he remained, to his death, adamantly opposed to concentration of wealth. The European aristocracy, based as it was on inherited wealth, was called "artificial" by Jefferson. "Provisions . . . to prevent its ascendency should be taken in America," he wrote. Jefferson was not opposed to what he called "natural aristocracy," based on merit rather than inherited wealth; but against the artificial aristocracy he could sharpen his pen in a manner reserved for few other subjects: "Do not be frightened into their surrender by the alarms of the timid, or the croakings of wealth against the ascendency of the people," Jefferson wrote to Samuel Kercheval July 12, 1812. One turn of Jefferson's pen characterized European society as one of riders and horses, another as wolves and sheep, still another as hammer and anvil. There was to be more to Jefferson's American amalgam than a pale imitation of Europe.

From Paris during 1785, Jefferson wrote: "You are perhaps curious to know how this new scene has struck a savage from the mountains of America."* The words recalled characterizations of Franklin by Europeans as the philosopher as savage. Both men, confronting the world from which their ancestors had come, fully realized how much America and its native inhabitants had changed them. Jefferson's reception of the Old World was not warm:

> *I find the general state of humanity here most deplorable. The truth of Voltaire's observation, offers itself perpetually, that every man here must be either the hammer or the anvil.*

---

* H. A. Washington, *The Writings of Thomas Jefferson* (New York: John C. Riker, 1854), Vol. I, p. 444.

It is a true picture of that country to which they say we shall pass hereafter, and where we are to see God and his angels in splendor, and crowds of the damned trampled under their feet. While the great mass of the people are thus suffering under physical and moral oppression . . . compare it with that degree of happiness which is enjoyed in America, by every class of people.

Europe had a few compensations, such as a lack of public drunkenness, and fine architecture, painting, and music, wrote Jefferson. All this, however, did not reduce class differences, nor spread the happiness of which Jefferson was so enamored.

As he had removed references to property from his critique of a French bill of rights, Jefferson offered other suggestions for reducing the disparity between classes that he saw there. One such suggestion was a very steep schedule of progressive taxation.

Back in America, the revolution had helped to absolve the new country of what emerging aristocracy it had. Many of them moved to Canada. About a year after he wrote the Declaration of Independence, Jefferson wrote to Franklin:

The people seem to have laid aside the monarchial, and taken up the republican government, with as much ease as would have attended their throwing off of an old, and putting on a new suit of clothes. Not a single throe has attended this important transformation. A half-dozen aristocratical gentlemen, agonizing under the loss of pre-eminence, have sometimes ventured their sarcasms on our political metamorphosis. They have been thought fitter objects of pity, than of punishment.

America, fusing the native peoples' state of nature and Europe's monarchial state into a unique, agrarian civilization, evolved its own institutions, and its own interests, distinct from either the Indian or the European. Late in his life, Jefferson wrote to President James Monroe that "America, North and South, has a set of interests distinct from those of Europe, and peculiarly her own."

Statements of Jefferson's such as that in his letter to Monroe and others like it were much later to be called into service by expansionists eager to justify their hunger for land and the lengths to which it drove them. In Jefferson's lifetime, however, they expressed the perceptions of a developing national identity *vis-à-vis* Europe. European scholarship, according to Jefferson, had produced no books that could be used as comprehensive guides to the kind of civil government he sought to erect in America: "There does not exist a good elementary work on the organization of society into civil government; I mean a work which presents one good and comprehensive view of the system of principles on which such an organization should be founded, according to the rights of nature." The same idea had been expressed in slightly different words many years earlier by Franklin.

Most of all, Jefferson loathed monarchy, the state that laid heavily across the backs of the people. As late as 1800, a quarter century after he wrote the Declaration of Independence, Jefferson was given to such statements as: "We have wonderful rumors here. One that the king of England is dead!" Comparing the oppression of the monarchial states he found in Europe with the way American Indians maintained social cohesion in their societies, Jefferson wrote in *Notes on the State of Virginia:* "Insomuch as it were made a question of whether no law, as among the savage Americans, or too much law, as among the civilized Europeans, submits man to the greater evil, one who has seen both conditions of existence would pronounce it to be the last; and that the sheep are happier of themselves, than under the care of the wolves."

Both Franklin and Jefferson believed that power provided temptations to corruption (to which European leaders had long ago succumbed) and that to keep the same thing from happening in America required mechanisms by which the people kept watch on their leaders to make sure that they remained servants, and did not yield to a natural inclination to become hammer to the popular anvil. Public opinion became central to the maintenance of liberty—a notion contrary to European governance of their day, but very similar to the Iroquois confederacy, where the war chiefs sat in the Grand Council with the express purpose of reporting back to the people on the behavior of their leaders.

Jefferson described the role of public opinion in American Indian society in *Notes on Virginia*. His description was remarkably similar to Franklin's. The native Americans, Jefferson wrote, had not

> Submitted themselves to any laws, any coercive power and shadow of government. The only controls are their manners, and the moral sense of right and wrong. . . . An offence against these is punished by contempt, by exclusion from society, or, where the cause is serious, as that of murder, by the individuals whom it concerns.

"Imperfect as this species of coercion may seem, crimes are very rare among them," Jefferson continued. Recapitulating Colden's remarks, as well as Franklin's, Jefferson developed his thought: "The principles of their society forbidding all compulsion, they are led by duty and to enterprise by personal influence and persuasion." Sharing with other founders of America the Enlightenment assumption that Indian societies (at least those as yet uncorrupted by Europeans) approximated a state of nature, Jefferson questioned the theory advanced by supporters of monarchy that government originated in a patriarchial, monarchial form. Having studied Indian societies, such as the Iroquois, which were matrilineal and democratic, Jefferson speculated that:

There is an error into which most of the speculators on government have fallen, and which the well-known state of society of our Indians ought, before now, to have corrected. In their hypothesis of the origin of government, they suppose it to have commenced in the patriarchial or monarchial form. Our Indians are evidently in that state of nature which has passed the association of a single family, and not yet submitted to authority of positive laws, or any acknowledged magistrate.

Public opinion, freedom of action and expression, and the consent of the governed played an important role in Jefferson's perception of Indian societies. The guideline that Jefferson drew from the Indian example (and which he earnestly promoted in the First Amendment) allowed freedom until it violated another's rights: "Every man, with them, is perfectly free to follow his own inclinations. But if, in doing this, he violates the rights of another, if the case be slight, he is punished by the disesteem of society or, as we say, public opinion; if serious, he is tomahawked as a serious enemy." Indian leaders relied on public opinion to maintain their authority: "Their leaders influence them by their character alone; they follow, or not, as they please him whose character for wisdom or war they have the highest opinion."

While public opinion was useful in keeping elected leaders from assuming the role of wolves over sheep, public opinion also was recognized by Jefferson as a safety valve. To repress it would invite armed revolution by a public alienated from its leaders. Jefferson could hardly deny a public insistent on overthrowing its leaders. Their right to do so was expressed in his Declaration of Independence. Writing to W. S. Smith November 17, 1787, Jefferson refuted assertions of some Europeans that America was suffering from anarchy:

What country can preserve its liberties if their rulers are not warned from time to time that their people preserve the spirit of resistance? Let them take arms. The remedy is to set them right as to facts, pardon and pacify them. . . . The tree of liberty must be refreshed from time to time with the blood of patriots and tyrants.

Displaying a rationality that had yet to be tested by tyrants' manipulation of public opinion, Jefferson wrote in 1801; "It is rare that the public sentiment decides immorally or unwisely and the individual who disagrees with it ought to examine well his own opinion." At least until he became President, and found the wrath of opinion directed at him from time to time, Jefferson expressed almost a naive faith in the wisdom of public opinion. Jefferson believed that states should be small in size to allow public opinion to function most efficiently. Leaders ought to be subject to impeachment; the entire governmental system could be impeached by force of arms if the people thought fit to do so. Public opinion could be called upon, in the Indians' fashion, to raise an army.

Like that of the Iroquois, Jefferson's concept of popular consent allowed for impeachment of officials who offended the principles of law; also similar to the Indian conception, Jefferson spoke and wrote frequently that the least government was the best. Jefferson objected when boundaries for new states were drawn so as to make them several times larger than some of the original colonies:

This is reversing the natural order of things. A tractable people may be governed in large bodies but, in proportion as they depart from this character, the extent of their government must be less. We see into what small divisions the Indians are obliged to reduce their societies.

Jefferson's writings indicate that he did not expect, nor encourage, Americans to be tractable people. Least of all did he expect them to submit to involuntary conscription for unjustified wars. Freedom from such was the natural order of things. Franklin showed a similar inclination in *Poor Richard* for 1734: "If you ride a horse, sit close and tight. If you ride a man, sit easy and light."

Franklin, Jefferson, and others in their time who combined politics and natural history intensively studied the history and prehistory of northwestern Europe as it had been before the coming of the Romans. Like the Celts and other tribal people of Germany and the British Isles who had lived, according to Jefferson, in societies that functioned much like the Indian polities he had observed in his own time: "The Anglo-Saxons had lived under customs and unwritten laws based upon the natural rights of man. . . ." The monarchy was imposed on top of this natural order, Jefferson argued. In so doing, according to Chinard, Jefferson "went much farther than any of the English political thinkers in his revindication of Saxon liberties." To Charles Sanford (*The Quest for Paradise*, 1961), America and its inhabitants represented to many Europeans a recapitulation of the Garden of Eden; to Henry Steele Commager, the Enlightenment mind assumed that "only man in a state of nature was happy. Man before the Fall." To English whigs, as well as to Franklin and Jefferson, government by the people was the wave of the past, as well as the future. Augmented by observation of Indian peoples who lived with a greater degree of happiness than peoples in Europe, this belief gave powerful force to the argument that the American Revolution was reclaiming rights that Americans, Englishmen, and all other peoples enjoyed by fiat of nature, as displayed by their ancestory—American Indian and European.

English radicals and American patriots traded these ideas freely across the Atlantic during the revolutionary years. One example of this intellectual trade was Tom Paine, who came to America at Franklin's invitation and within three years of his arrival was sitting around a council fire with the Iroquois, learning to speak their language and enjoying himself very much. Paine attended a treaty council at Easton during 1777, in order to negotiate the Iroquois' alliance, or at least neutrality, in the Revolutionary War. According to Samuel Edwards, a biographer of Paine, he was "fascinated by them." Paine quickly learned enough of the Iroquois' language so that he no longer needed to speak through an interpreter.

It was not long before Paine, like Jefferson and Franklin, was contrasting the Indians' notions of property with those of the Europe from which he had come. Paine not only demoted property from the roster of natural rights and made of it a mere device of civil society, but also recognized benefits in the Indians' communal traditions:

> To understand what the state of society ought to be, it is necessary to have some idea of the natural and primitive state of man; such as it is at this day among the Indians of North America. There is not, in that state, any of those spectacles of human misery which poverty and want present to our eyes in all the towns and streets of Europe.

Poverty, wrote Paine 1795, "is a thing created by what is called civilization." "Civilization, or that which is so called, has operated in two ways: to make one part of society more affluent, and the other more wretched, than would ever have been the lot of either in a natural state," Paine concluded. Despite the appeal of a society without poverty, Paine believed it impossible "to go from the civilized to the natural state."

The rationale for revolution that was formulated in Philadelphia during those humid summer days of 1776 threw down an impressive intellectual gauntlet at the feet of Europe's monarchies, especially the British Crown. Franklin, Jefferson, and the others who drafted the Declaration of Independence were saying that they were every inch the equal of the monarchs who would superintend them, and that the sheep of the world had a natural right to smite the wolves, a natural right guaranteed by nature, by the precedent of their ancestors, and by the abundant and pervasive example of America's native inhabitants. The United States' founders may have read about Greece, or the Roman Republic, the cantons of the Alps, or the reputed democracy of the tribal Celts, but in the Iroquois and other Indian confederacies they saw, with their own eyes, the self-evidence of what they regarded to be irrefutable truths.

Wars are not won soley by eloquence and argument, however. Once he had recovered from the gout, Franklin recalled his talents at organizing militias and threw himself into the practical side of organizing an armed struggle for independence. He marshaled brigades that went house to house with appeals for pots, pans, and curtain weights, among other things, which would be melted down to provide the revolutionary army with ammunition. The colonists set to work raising a volunteer army in the Indian manner (much as Franklin had organized his Philadelphia militia almost three decades earlier), using Indian battle tactics so well suited to the forests of eastern North America. George Washington had studied guerrilla warfare during the war with France, and when the British sent soldiers over the ocean ready for set-piece wars on flat pastures manicured like billiard tables, their commanders wailed that Washington's army was just not being fair— shooting from behind trees, dispersing and returning to civilian occupations when opportunity or need called. A British Army report to the House of Commons exclaimed, in exasperation, "The Americans won't stand and fight!"

Having failed to adapt to a new style of war in a new land, the British never exactly lost the war, but like another world power that sent its armies across an ocean two centuries later, they decided they could not win a war without fronts, without distinction between soldiers and civilians. America would have its independence.

Meeting in Paris to settle accounts during 1783, the diplomats who redrew the maps sliced the Iroquois Confederacy in half, throwing a piece to the United States, and another to British Canada. The heirs to some of the Great Law of Peace's most precious principles ignored the Iroquois' protestations that they, too, were sovereign nations, deserving independence and self-determination. A century of learning was coming to a close. A century and more of forgetting—of calling history into service to rationalize conquest—was beginning.

AFTERWORD

The Indians presented a reverse image of European civilization which helped America establish a national identity that was neither savage nor civilized.
—Charles Sanford, The Quest for Paradise, 1961

From the beginning of European contact with the Americas, a kind of intellectual mercantilism seemed to take shape. Like the economic mercantilism that drew raw materials from the colonies, made manufactured goods from them in Europe, and then sold the finished products back to America, European savants drew the raw material of observation and perception from America, fashioned it into theories, and exported those theories back across the Atlantic. What role, it may be asked, did these observations of America and its native inhabitants play in the evolution of Enlightenment thought in Europe? "The Indians," wrote Charles Sanford with credit to Roy Harvey Pearce, "presented a reverse image of European civilization which helped America establish a national identity which was neither savage nor civilized." How true was this also of Europe itself? During the researching of the foregoing study, the author came across shreds of evidence which, subsequently not followed because they fell outside the range of the study, indicate that European thinkers such as John Locke, Jean Jacques Rousseau, and others may have drawn from America and its native inhabitants observations on natural society, natural law, and natural rights, packaged them into theories, and exported them back to America, where people such as Franklin and Jefferson put them into practice in construction of their American amalgam.

In *The Quest for Paradise*, Sanford drew a relation between American Indians' conception of property and that expressed by Thomas More in his *Utopia*. Paul A. W. Wallace also likened the Iroquois' governmental structure to that of *Utopia*. Work could be done that would begin with the basis laid by Sanford, Robert F. Berkhofer, and Roy Harvey Pearce, which would examine how Europeans such as Locke and other seventeenth and eighteenth-century philosophers integrated observation and perception of American Indians into theories of natural rights. Michael Kraus (*The Atlantic Civilization*, 1949) wrote that during this period, anthropology was strongly influencing the development of political theory: "[Thomas] Hobbes and Locke, especially, show a familiarity with the social structure of the American Indians which they used to good purpose. Each of the English political scientists wrote in a period of crisis and in search of a more valid ordering of society. . . . The American Indian was believed to have found many of the answers." If such intellectual intercourse did, in fact, occur, how did the Europeans get their information? How accurate was it? What other non-Indian precedents did they use in formulating their theories? How were these theories exported back to America, which, as Commager observed, acted the Enlightenment that Europe dreamed? Berkhofer quoted Locke as having written: "In the beginning, all the world was America." According to Berkhofer, Locke believed that men could live in reason and peace without European-style government; Berkhofer implied that Locke saw proof of this, as Jefferson and Franklin did, in the societies of the American Indians. Koch wrote that the English radicals of the eighteenth century were "students and advocates" of the American cause. Franklin, with his rich, firsthand knowledge of Indians and their societies, was well known in England before he began work there in the 1750s. Gillespie wrote that England had been suffused with influences from America, material as well as intellectual, as part of its rapid overseas expansion of empire. Gillespie noted Indian influences in More's *Utopia* and in Hobbes's *Leviathan.* Gillespie also found similar relationships in Locke's writings.

In France, reports of Indian societies traveled to the home country through the writings of Jesuit missionaries, among other channels. How might such writings have influenced the conceptions of natural rights and law developed by Rousseau and others? Frank Kramer has described how some ideas were transmitted home from New France. As the Indians' societies became a point of reference for natural rights theorists in England, so did conceptions of the "Noble Savage" in France. More study needs to be done to document how these ideas, and others, made their way across the Atlantic and into the intellectual constructs of Rousseau and others who helped excite the French imagination in the years preceding the revolution of 1789.

Carried into the nineteenth century, study could be given to whether American Indian ideas had any bearing on the large number of social and political reform movements that developed during the 1830s and 1840s in the "burned over district" of western New York. That area had been the heart of the Iroquois Confederacy a hundred years earlier, when Colden was writing his history of the Iroquois. Do the origins of the anti-slavery movement, of women's rights, and religions such as Mormonism owe anything to the Iroquois?

Two contemporaries of Buffalo Bill, Karl Marx and Frederich Engels, about the time of the Custer Battle were drawing on the

Indian models to support their theories of social evolution. As had Franklin and Jefferson a century before, Marx and Engels paid particular attention to the lack of state-induced coercion and the communal role of property that operated in the Iroquois Confederacy.

Marx read Lewis Henry Morgan's *Ancient Society,* which had been published in 1877, between December 1880 and March 1881, taking at least ninety-eight pages of handwritten notes. *Ancient Society* was Morgan's last major work; his first book-length study had been *The League of the Ho-de-no-sau-nee or Iroquois* (1851). Morgan was a close friend of the Seneca Ely Parker, a high-ranking Civil War officer. Like Johnson, Weiser, Colden, and others, Morgan was an adopted Iroquois. When Marx read Morgan's *Ancient Society,* he and Engels were studying the important anthropologists of their time. Morgan was one of them.

Marx's notes on *Ancient Society* adhere closely to the text, with little extraneous comment. What particularly intrigued Marx about the Iroquois was their democratic political organization, and how it was meshed with a communal economic system—how, in short, economic leveling was achieved without coercion.

During the late 1870s and early 1880s, Marx remained an insatiable reader, but a life of poverty and attendant health problems had eroded his ability to organize and synthesize what he had read. After Marx died, Engels inherited his notes and, in 1884, published *The Origin of the Family, Private Property and the State,* subtitled *In Light of the Researches of Lewis H. Morgan.* The book sold well; it had gone through four editions in German by 1891. Engels called the book a "bequest to Marx." He wrote that Morgan's account of the Iroquois Confederacy "substantiated the view that classless communist societies had existed among primitive peoples," and that these societies had been free of some of the evils, such as class stratification, that he associated with industrial capitalism. Jefferson had been driven by similar evils to depict Europe in metaphors of wolves and sheep, hammer and anvil.

To Engels, Morgan's description of the Iroquois was important because "it gives us the opportunity of studying the organization of a society which, as yet, knows no state." Jefferson had also been interested in the Iroquois' ability to maintain social consensus without a large state apparatus, as had Franklin. Engels described the Iroquoian state in much the same way that American revolutionaries had a century earlier:

> Everything runs smoothly without soldiers, gendarmes, or police, without nobles, kings, governors, prefects or judges; without prisons, without trials. All quarrels and disputes are settled by the whole body of those concerned. . . . The household is run communistically by a number of families; the land is tribal property, only the small gardens being temporarily assigned to the households—still, not a bit of our extensive and complicated machinery of administration is required. . . . There are no poor and needy. The communistic household and the gens know their responsibility toward the aged, the sick and the disabled in war. All are free and equal—including the women.

Concern for the depredations of human rights by state power is no less evident in our time than in the eighteenth century. American Indians, some of the earliest exemplars of those rights, today often petition the United Nations for redress of abuses committed by the United States government, whose founding declarations often ring hollow in ears so long calloused by the thundering horsehooves of Manifest Destiny and its modern equivalents. One may ask what the United Nations' declarations of human rights owe to the Iroquois and other Indian nations. Take the following excerpts from the United Nations Universal Declaration of Human Rights (adopted December 10, 1948), and place them next to the Great Law of Peace, and the statements Franklin and other American national fathers adapted from experience with American Indian nations:

> *All human beings are born free and equal in dignity and rights. They are endowed with reason and conscience and should act toward one another in a spirit of brotherhood. (Article 1)*

> *Every person has a right to life, liberty and security of person. (Article 3)*

> *Everyone has a right to freedom of thought, conscience and religion. (Article 18)*

> *Everyone has the right of freedom of opinion and religion. (Article 19)*

> *. . . The will of the people shall be the basis of the authority of governments . . . (Article 21)*

Looking across the frontier, as well as across the Atlantic, looking at Indian peace as well as Indian wars, history poses many tantalizing questions. The thesis that American Indian thought played an important role in shaping the mind of European America, and of Europe itself, is bound to incite controversy, a healthy state of intellectual affairs at any time in history, our own included. The argument around which this book is centered is only one part of a broader effort not to rewrite history, but to expand it, to broaden our knowledge beyond the intellectual strait jacket of ethnocentricism that tells us that we teach, but we do not learn from, peoples and cultures markedly different from our own.

Fortunately, there are fresh winds stirring. Dr. Jeffry Goodman has started what one reviewer called a "civil war" in archaeology.

Dr. Henry Dobyns's mathematically derived estimate that 90 million Indians lived in the Americas prior to the arrival of Columbus has also stirred debate. There is a sense that we are only beginning to grasp the true dimensions of American history to which Europeans have been personal witness only a few short centuries. The Europeans who migrated here are still learning the history of their adopted land, and that of the peoples who flourished here (and who themselves are today rediscovering their own magnificent pasts). In a very large sense we are only now beginning to rediscover the history that has been passed down in tantalizing shreds, mostly through the oral histories of Indian nations that have survived despite the best efforts of some Euro-Americans to snuff out Indian languages, cultures, and the land base that gives all sustenance. History in its very essence is rediscovery, and we are now relearning some of the things that Benjamin Franklin and others of our ancestors had a chance to see, feel, remark at, and integrate into their view of the world.

The United States was born during an era of Enlightenment that recognized the universality of humankind, a time in which minds and borders were opened to the new, the wondrous, and the unexpected. It was a time when the creators of a nation fused the traditions of Europe and America, appreciating things that many people are only now rediscovering—the value of imagery and tradition shaped by oral cultures that honed memory and emphasized eloquence, that made practical realities of democratic principles that were still the substance of debate (and, to some, heresy) in Europe. In its zest for discovery, the Enlightenment mind absorbed Indian traditions and myth, and refashioned it, just as Indians adopted the ways of European man. In this sense, we are all heirs to America's rich Indian heritage.

Like the eighteenth-century explorers who looked westward from the crests of the Appalachians, we too stand at the edge of a frontier of another kind, wondering with all the curiosity that the human mind can summon what we will find over the crest of the hill in the distance, or around the bend in the river we have yet to see for the first time. What will America teach us next?

BIBLIOGRAPHY

A Note on the Bibliography

With a view to rendering some assistance to the interested reader, this bibliography has been divided into five sections: sources concerned with the subject as a whole, those more specifically concerned with the Iroquois culture, two sections concerned respectively with sources reflecting Franklin's and Jefferson's contact with the Indians, and a final section of sources useful, chiefly, in the writing of the afterword.

These sections are further subdivided into primary and secondary sources and into published and unpublished material.

For the benefit of readers who wish to know if a certain author has been consulted, a separate index of authors' names will be found at the end of the bibliography.

BIBLIOGRAPHY

General Background

FINDING AIDS

Freeman, John F. *A Guide to Manuscripts Relating to the American Indian in the Library of the American Philosophical Society.* Philadelphia: American Philosophical Society, 1965.

Museum of the American Indian (Heye Foundation) New York City. "Indian Notes and Monographs, No. 49." New York: Museum of the American Indian, 1957.

Museum of the American Indian (Heye Foundation) New York City. *List of Publications of the Museum of the American Indian.* 9th ed. New York: Musuem of the American Indian, 1957.

SECONDARY SOURCES

Articles and Other Short Monographs

————. "Our Indian Heritage." *Life,* July 2, 1971.

Ackernecht, Edwin H. "White Indians." *Bulletin of the History of Medicine* 15(1944):8–26.

Brandon, William. "American Indians and American History." *American West,* Spring 1965, pp. 14–26.

Cohen, Felix. "Americanizing the White Man." *American Scholar* 21:2(1952):177–191.

Cook, S.F. "Demographic Consequences of European Contact With Primitive Peoples." *Annals of the American Academy of Political and Social Sciences* 237(1945):107–111.

Edwards, Everett E. "The Contributions of American Indians to Civilization." *Minnesota History* 15:3(1934):255–272.

Ewers, John C. "When Red and White Men Meet." *Western Historical Quarterly* 2:2(1971):133–150.

Fenton, William N. "Contacts Between Iroquois Herbalism and Colonial Medicine." *Smithsonian Institution Report.* [1941]. Washington, D.C.: Government Printing Office, 1941.

Fife, Austin E. "The Pseudo-Indian Folksongs of the Anglo-American and French Canadian." *Journal of American Folklore* 67(1954).

Frachtenberg, Leo J. "Our Indebtedness to the American Indian." *Wisconsin Archeologist* 14:2(1915):64–69.

Gibson, A.M. "Sources for Research on the American Indian." *Ethnohistory* 7:2(1962):121–136.

Bibliography

Hallowell, A. Irving. "The Backwash of the Frontier: The Impact of the Indian on American Culture." Edited by Walker D. Wyman and Clifton B. Kroeber. *The Frontier in Perspective*. Madison: University of Wisconsin Press, 1957.

——. "The Impact of the American Indian on American Culture." *American Anthropologist*. New Series 59:2(1957):201–207.

Hayes, Carlton J.H. "The American Frontier—Frontier of What?" *American Historical Review* 51:1(1946):199–216.

Hofstadter, Richard. "Turner and the Frontier Myth." *American Scholar* 18:3(1949):433–443.

Kramer, Lucy M. "Indian Contributions to American Culture." *Indians Yesterday and Today*. Washington, D.C.: United States Department of Interior, (1941).

Larrabee, Edward M. "Recurrent Themes and Sequences in North American Indian-European Culture Contact." *American Philosophical Transactions Society* 66:7(1976).

Miller, Walter B. "Two Concepts of Authority." *American Anthropologist*. New Series 62:2(1955):271–289.

Morey, Sylvester M. "American Indians and Our Way of Life." *Myron Proceedings* Institute: Adelphi College 13(1961):4–28.

Safford, William E. "Our Heritage from the American Indians." *Smithsonian Institution Annual Report*. [1926]. Washington, D.C.: Government Printing Office, 1927.

Stirling, Matthew W. "America's First Settlers: The Indians." *National Geographic*, November 1937, p. 535.

Udall, Stewart L. "Indians: First Americans, First Ecologists." *The American Way*, May 1971, pp. 8–12.

Books and Longer Monographs

Armstrong, Virginia. *I Have Spoken: American History Through the Eyes of American Indians*. Chicago: Swallow Press, 1971.

Berkhofer, Robert F. *The White Man's Indian: Images of the American Indian From Columbus to the Present*. New York: Afred A. Knopf, 1977.

Bohannan, Paul and Fred Plog, eds. *Beyond the Frontier: Social Process and Cultural Change*. New York: American Museum of Natural History, 1967.

Carter, E. Russell. *The Gift is Rich*. New York: Friendship Press, 1955.

Chamberlin, J.E. *The Harrowing of Eden: White Attitudes Toward Native Americans*. New York: Seabury Press, 1975.

Cohen, Lucy Kramer, ed. *The Legal Conscience: Selected Papers of Felix S. Cohen*. New Haven: Yale University Press, 1960.

Cohen, Morris R. and Cohen, Felix S. *Readings in Jurisprudence and Legal Philosophy*. Boston: Little Brown and Co., 1951.

Crosby, Alfred W. *The Columbian Exchange: Biological and Cultural Consequences of 1492*. Westport, Conn.: Greenwood Press, 1972.

Forbes, Jack. *The Indian in America's Past*. Englewood Cliffs, N.J.: Prentice-Hall, Inc., 1964.

Gillespie, James E. *The Influence of Overseas Expansion on England to 1700*. New York: Longmans, Green & Co., 1920.

Hanke, Lewis. *Aristotle and the American Indian: A Study in Race Prejudice in the Modern World*. [1950]. Bloomington; Indiana University Press, 1975.

James, George W. *What the White Race May Learn from the Indian.* Chicago: Forbes & Co., 1908.

Johansen, Bruce E. and Roberto Maestas. *Wasi'chu: The Continuing Indian Wars.* New York: Monthly Review Press, 1979.

Kramer, Frank R. *Voices in the Valley.* Madison: University of Wisconsin Press, 1964.

Lips, Julian. *The Savage Hits Back.* New Haven: Yale University Press, 1937.

Locke, Alain and Bernhard J. Stern, eds. *When Peoples Meet: A Study in Race and Culture Contacts.* New York: Hinds, Hayden and Eldredge, 1946.

Pruca, Francis Paul. *American Indian Policy in the Formative Years.* Cambridge: Harvard University Press, 1962.

Quimby, George Irving. *Indian Culture and European Trade Goods: The Archeology of the Historic Period in the Western Great Lakes Region.* Madison: University of Wisconsin Press, 1966.

Readers Digest. "Our Fascinating Indian Heritage." Pleasantville, N.Y.: Readers Digest Association, 1979.

Saum, Lewis O. *The Fur Trader and the Indian.* Seattle: University of Washington Press, 1965.

Sheehan, Bernhard. *Seeds of Extinction.* Chapel Hill: University of North Carolina Press, 1973.

Vogel, Virgil J. *This Country Was Ours.* New York: Harper & Row, 1972.

———. *The Indian in American History.* Chicago: Integrated Education Associates, 1968.

Wilson, Edmund. *Apologies to the Iroquois.* New York: Farrar, Straus & Cudahy, 1960.

Wright, Lewis B. *Culture on the Moving Frontier.* Bloomington: Indiana University Press, 1955.

Yawser, Rose N. *The Indian and the Pioneer: An Historical Perspective.* Syracuse, N.Y.: C.W. Bardeen, 1893.

Zolla, Elemire. *The Writer and the Shaman: A Morphology of the American Indian.* New York: Harcourt, Brace, Jovanovich, 1973.

The Iroquois and Early Colonial Contact

FINDING AIDS

Brown, Jessie Louise P. *A Bibliography of the Iroquois Indians.* M.A. thesis, Columbia University, 1903.

Dockstader, Frederick J. *The American Indian in Graduate Studies: A Bibliography of Theses and Dissertations.* New York: Museum of the American Indian, Heye Foundation, 1957.

Fenton, William N. "A Calendar of Manuscript Materials Relating to the History of the Six Nations or Iroquois in Depositories Outside Philadelphia 1750–1850." *Proceedings.* American Philosophical Society 97:5(1957): 578–595.

Freeman, John F. *A Guide to Manuscripts Relating to the American Indian in the Library of the American Philosophical Society.* Philadelphia: American Philosophical Society, 1966.

Bibliography

Snyderman, George S. "A Preliminary Survey of American Indian Manuscripts in Repositories of the Philadelphia Area." *Proceedings*. American Philosophical Society 97:5(1957):596–610.

PRIMARY SOURCES

Published Primary Sources

————. *The Great Law of Peace of the Longhouse People*. Rooseveltown, N.Y.: *Akwesasne Notes* and Mohawk Nation, 1977.

Bartram, John. *A Journey from Pensilvania to Onondage in 1743*. Barre, Mass.: Imprint Society, 1973.

————. *Travels in Pennsilvania and Canada* [1751]. Ann Arbor, Mich.: University Microfilms, 1966.

Colden, Cadwallader. *The History of the Five Indian Nations Depending on the Province of New York in America.* [1727 and 1747]. Ithaca, N.Y.: Cornell University Press, 1958.

————. *The History of the Five Indian Nations of Canada.* [1765]. New York: New Amsterdam Book Co., 1902.

————. *The Letters and Papers of Cadwallader Colden*. Collections of the New York Historical Society. 1917–1923 and 1934–1935.

Cusick, David. *Ancient History of the Six Nations.* Lockport, N.Y.: Niagara County Historical Society 1824.

Fenton, William N., ed. *Parker on the Iroquois*. Syracuse, N.Y.: Syracuse University Press, 1968.

Heckewelder, John. *History, Manners and Customs of the Indian Nations Who Once Inhabited Pennsylvania and the Neighboring States.* [1819]. New York: Arno Press, 1971.

Johnston, Charles M., ed. *The Valley of the Six Nations.* Toronto: University of Toronto Press, 1964.

Leder, Lawrence H., ed. *The Livingston Indian Records 1666–1725.* Gettysburg, Penn.: Pennsylvania Historical Association, 1956.

Morgan, Lewis Henry. *League of the Ho-de-no-sau-nee or Iroquois.* [1851]. New York: Dodd, Mead & Co., 1902.

————. (Shenandoah). "Letters on the Iroquois." *American Review* (1847): February, pp. 8–18; March, pp. 242–256; May, pp. 447–461.

Proctor, Thomas. *Narrative of a Journey of Col. Thomas Proctor to the Indians of the Northwest.* In *Pennsylvania Archives*, Second Series, vol. 44:551–662.

Schoolcraft, Henry R. *Algic Researches: Comprising Inquiries Respecting the Mental Characteristics of North American Indians.* New York: Harper & Bros., 1859.

————. *The American Indians: Their History, Culture and Prospects.* Buffalo, N.Y.: Rochester, Wanzer & Co., 1851.

————. *Historical and Statistical Information Respecting the History, Conditions and Prospects of the Indians in the United States.* 6 vols. Philadelphia: Lippincott, Grambo, 1851–1857.

————. *Personal Memoirs of Thirty Years With the Indian Tribes on the American Frontiers . . . A.D. 1812 to A.D. 1842.* Philadelphia: Lippincott, 1851.

The Iroquois and Early Colonial Contact

————. Notes on the Iroquois or Contributions to the Statistics, Aboriginal History, Antiquities and General Ethnology of Western New York. New York: Bartlett and Welford, 1846.

Smith, William, Jr. A History of the Province of New York. Edited by Michael Kammen. [2 vols.: 1751 and 1824]. New Haven: Yale University Press, 1972.

Snowden, James R. The Cornplanter Memorial: Published by Order of the Legislature of Pennsylvania. Harrisburg, Penn.: Singerly & Myers, State Printers, 1867.

Weiser, Conrad. Narrative of a Journey from Tulpehocken, in Pennsylvania, to Onondago, the Headquarters of the Six Nations of Indians . . . in 1737. Philadelphia: J. Pennington, 1853.

Unpublished Primary Sources

Fadden, Ray. Iroquois Past and Present in the State of New York. [1949]. Typescript, American Philosophical Society, Philadelphia.

Hewitt, J. N. B. "A Constitutional League of Peace in the Stone Age of America: The League of the Iroquois and its Constitution." [1918]. Washington, D.C.: National Anthropological Archives, Smithsonian Institution.

————. "Constitution of the Iroquois League." No date. Washington, D.C.: National Anthropological Archives. Smithsonian Institution.

————. "The Constitution of the Five Nations." [1916]. Washington, D.C.: National Anthropological Archives, Smithsonian Institution.

————. "The Founding of the League of the Five Nations by Deganawidah." No Date. Washington, D.C.: National Anthropological Archives, Smithsonian Institution.

————. "Status of Women in the Iroquois Polity Before 1784." [1933]. Washington, D.C.: National Anthropological Archives, Smithsonian Institution.

Newhouse, Seth. "Constutution of the Five Nations' Indian Confederation." [1880]. Washington, D.C.: National Anthropological Archives, Smithsonian Institution.

————. Cosmology of De-ka-na-wi-da's Government. [1885]. Philadelphia: American Philosophical Society.

Parker, Arthur C. "The American Indian, the Government and the Country." [1915]. New York City Public Library.

Shea, J.G. "Sketch of the History of the Iroquois." [1896]. Washington, D.C.: National Anthropological Archives, Smithsonian Institution.

SECONDARY SOURCES

Published Secondary Sources

ARTICLES AND OTHER SHORT MONOGRAPHS

Bauman, Robert F. "Claims vs. Realities: The Anglo-Iroquois Partnership." Northwest Ohio Quarterly 32:2(1960):87–101.

Beauchamp, William M. "Morovian Journals Relating to Central New York 1745–1766." Syracuse, N.Y.: Onondaga Historical Association, 1916.

Blau, Harold. "Historical Factors in Onondaga Iroquois Cultural Stability." Ethnohistory 12:2(1965):250–258.

Carse, Mary R. "The Mohawk Iroquois." Bulletin of the Archeological Society of Connecticut 23(1942):3–53.

Bibliography

Decker, George P. "Must the Peaceful Iroquois Go?" Rochester, N.Y.: Lewis H. Morgan Chapter, 1928.

Fenton, William N. "Collecting Materials for a Political History of the Six Nations." *Proceedings* American Philosophical Society 93:3(1949):233–238.

――――. "Seth Newhouse's Traditional History and Constitution of the Iroquois Confederacy." *Proceedings* American Philosophical Society 93:3(1949): 141–158.

――――. "Locality as a Basic Factor in the Development of Iroquois Social Structure." *Bulletin* Bureau of American Ethnology 149(1952).

Hayes, Carlton J.H. "The American Frontier—Frontier of What?" *American Historical Review* 51:2(1946):199–216.

Howard, Helen A. "Hiawatha—Cofounder of an Indian United Nations." *Journal of the West* 10:3(1971):428–438.

Jacobs, Wilbur R. "Wampum: The Protocol of Indian Diplomacy." *William and Mary Quarterly* 3rd series 4:3(1949):596–604.

Morgan, William T. "The Five Nations and Queen Anne." *Mississippi Valley Historical Review* 13(1927):169–189.

Root, Elihu. "The Iroquois and the Struggle for America: Address on the Tercentennial Celebration of the Discovery of Lake Champlain, Plattsburg, N.Y., July 7, 1909." Washington, D.C.: Sudwarth Printing Co., 1909.

Schlesinger, Arthur M. "Liberty Tree: A Genealogy." *New England Quarterly* 25(1952):435–458.

Sherman, Daniel. "The Six Nations: An Address Delivered Before the Chataqua Society, Jamestown, N.Y., January 29, 1855." New York: no publisher, 1855.

Speck, Frank G. "The Iroquois: A Study in Cultural Evolution." Bloomfield Hills, Mich.: Cranbrook Institute of Science, *Bulletin* 23, October, 1945.

Tooker, Elizabeth. "Northern Iroquian Sociopolitical Organization." *American Anthropologist* 72:1(1970):90–96.

Wallace, Paul A.W. "The Return of Hiawatha." *New York State History* 39(1948):385–403.

Wintemberg, William J. "Distinguishing Characteristics of Algonkin and Iroquoian Cultures." Canadian Department of Mines, National Museum of Canada *Annual Report* [1929], pp. 65–124.

Wroth, Lawrence C. "The Indian Treaty as Literature." *Yale Review* 17(1927–1928):749–766.

BOOKS AND LONGER MONOGRAPHS

――――. *The History of Brant, Ontario . . . Early Settlers . . . History of the Six Nations.* Toronto: Warner, Beers & Co., 1883.

――――. *The Influence of the Iroquois on the History and Archeology of the Wyoming Valley, Pennsylvania and Adjacent Region.* Wilkes-Barre, Penn.: Wyoming Historical and Geological Society, 1911.

Beauchamp, William M. *A History of the New York Iroquois, Now Commonly Called the Six Nations.* Port Washington, N.Y.: I.J. Friedman, 1962.

Blanchard, Rufus. *The Iroquois Confederacy.* Chicago: R. Blanchard, 1902.

Brodhead, John R. *History of the State of New York.* 2 vols. New York: Harper & Bros., 1871.

Carr, Lucien. *The Social and Political Position of Women Among The Huron-Iroquois Tribes.* Salem, Mass.: Salem Press, 1884.

Donohue, Thomas. *The Iroquois and the Jesuits.* Buffalo, N.Y.: Buffalo Catholic Publishing Co., 1895.

Fadden, Ray (Aren Akweks). *The Formation of the Ho-de-no-sau-nee or League of the Five Nations*. Hogansburg, N.Y.: Akwesasne Counsellor Organization, 1948.

Fenton, William N. *Symposium on Local Diversity in Iroquois Culture*. Washington, D.C.: Government Printing Office, 1951.

Hale, Horatio E. *The Iroquois Book of Rites*. Toronto: University of Toronto Press, 1963.

Huntington, Ellsworth. *The Red Man's Continent: A Chronicle of Aboriginal America*. New Haven: Yale University Press, 1921.

Jennings, Francis. *The Invasion of America: Indians, Colonialism and the Cant of Conquest*. Chapel Hill: University of North Carolina Press, 1975.

Johnson, Anna C. *The Iroquois, or the Bright Side of Indian Character*. New York: D. Appleton & Co., 1855.

Kimm, Silas C. *The Iroquois: A History of the Six Nations of New York*. Middleburgh, N.Y.: P.W. Danforth, 1900.

Klein, Milton, *The Politics of Diversity: Essays in the History of Colonial New York*. Port Washington, N.Y.: Kennikat Press, 1974.

Kriegal, Leonard. *Edmund Wilson*. Carbondale: Southern Illinois University Press, 1971.

Leder, Lawrence H. *Robert Livingston 1654–1728 and the Politics of Colonial New York*. Chapel Hill: University of North Carolina Press, 1961.

Marsden, Michael T. *A Selected Annotated Edition of Henry Schoolcraft's Personal Memoirs of a Residence of Thirty Years With the Indian Tribes of North America*. Bowling Green, Ohio: Bowling Green University, 1972.

Morgan, Edmund S. *The Mirror of the Indian: An Exhibition of Books and Other Source Materials*. Providence, R.I.: The Associates of the John Carter Brown Library, 1958.

Moultrop, Samuel P. *Iroquois*. Rochester, N.Y.: E. Hart, 1901.

Parker, Arthur C. *An Analytical History of the Seneca Indians*. Rochester, N.Y.: Lewis H. Morgan Chapter, 1926.

———. *The Life of General Ely S. Parker*. Buffalo, N.Y.: Buffalo Historical Society Publications, 1905.

Pearce, Roy Harvey. *The Savages of America: A Study of the Indian and the Idea of Civilization*. Baltimore: Johns Hopkins University Press, 1965.

Reaman, G. Elmore. *Trail of the Iroquois Indians: How the Iroquois Saved Canada for the British Empire*. New York: Barnes & Noble, 1967.

Ritchie, William A. *Indian History of New York State*. Albany: New York State Museum, 1953.

Ruttenber, E.M. *The History of the Indian Tribes of Hudson's River*. [1872]. Port Washington, N.Y.: Kennikat Press, 1971.

Strickland, Edward D. *Iroquois Past and Present*. Buffalo: A.M.S. Press, 1901.

Trelease, Allen W. *Indian Affairs in Colonial New York: The Seventeenth Century*. [1960]. Port Washington, N.Y.: Kennikat Press, 1971.

Tooker, Elizabeth, ed. *Iroquois Culture, History and Prehistory: Proceedings of a Conference on Iroquois Research, Glens Falls, N.Y.*, 1965. Albany: New York State Education Department, 1967.

Underhill, Ruth M. *Red Man's Continent: A History of the Indians in the United States*. Chicago: University of Chicago Press, 1953.

Vanderwerth, W. *Indian Oratory*. Norman: University of Oklahoma Press, 1971.

Bibliography

Wallace, Paul A.W. *Indians in Pennsylvania.* Harrisburg, Penn.: The Pennsylvania Historical and Museum Commission, 1961.
————. *The White Roots of Peace.* Philadelphia: University of Pennsylvania Press, 1946.
Wissler, Clark. *Indians of the United States: Four Centuries of Their History and Culture.* Garden City, N.Y.: Doubleday, 1953.

Unpublished Secondary Sources

THESES AND DISSERTATIONS

Aquila, Richard. *The Iroquois Restoration: A Study of Iroquois Power, Politics and Relations With Indians and Whites.* Ph.D. dissertation, Ohio State University, 1961.
Bramson, Emily K. *New York State and the Iroquois Indians.* M.A. thesis, Columbia University, 1940.
Bridge, Beatrice M. *The Influence of the Iroquois on the Development of New France.* M.A. thesis, Saskatchewan University, 1938.
Clarke-Smith, Linda. *Primitive Women: A Study of Women Among Tribes of Australia and the Iroquois Confederacy.* M.A. thesis, Columbia University, 1907.
Clingan, Dorothy E. *The Iroquois Confederacy 1682–1690.* M.A. thesis, Yale University, 1934.
Coogan, John E. *The Eloquence of Our American Indians.* Ph.D. dissertation, St. Louis University, 1923.
Foley, Dennis. *An Ethnographic Analysis of the Iroquois.* Ph.D. dissertation, State University of New York at Albany, 1955.
Gerken, Walter D. *The Relation of the Iroquois in the Struggle Between the French and the English in North America.* M.A. thesis, Columbia University, 1902.
Jaffe, Herman J. *The Iroquois Confederacy in the Wars of the Iroquois.* M.A. thesis, Columbia University, 1961.
MacLeod, William C. *The Origin of the State Reconsidered in the Light of the Data of Aboriginal North America.* Ph.D. dissertation, University of Pennsylvania, 1924.
Newell, William B. *Crime and Justice Among the Iroquois Indians.* M.A. thesis, University of Pennsylvania, 1934.
Noon, John A. *The League of the Iroquois on Grand River: An Acculturation Study in Government and Law.* Ph.D. dissertation, University of Pennsylvania, 1942.
Preska, Margaret R. *Speech Communication in the Iroquois Confederacy.* M.A. thesis, Pennsylvania State University, 1961.
Reynolds, Wynn R. *Persuasive Speaking of the Iroquois at Treaty Councils 1678–1776: A Study of Techniques as Evidenced in the Offical Transcripts of the Interpreters' Translations.* Ph.D. dissertation, Columbia University, 1957.
Richards, Cara E. *The Role of Iroquois Women: A Study of the Onondaga Reservation.* Ph.D. dissertation, Cornell University, 1957.
Walsh, Joseph. *The Iroquois Confederacy: Unresolved Dilemma of American History.* M.A. thesis, Columbia University, 1965.
Wardy, Ben Z. *Iroquoian Government.* M.A. thesis, The New School, 1956.

Benjamin Franklin

FINDING AIDS

Bridgewater, Dorothy. "Notable Additions to the Franklin Collection." *Yale University Library Gazette* 20(1945):21–28.

Bell, Whitfield J., Jr. and Murphy D. Smith. *Guide to the Archives and Manuscript Collections of the American Philosophical Society.* Philadelphia: American Philosophical Society, 1966.

Day, Richard E., ed. *Calendar of Sir William Johnson Manuscripts in the New York State Library, Albany.* Albany: State of New York, 1909.

De Puy, Henry F. *A Bibliography of the English Colonial Treaties With the Indians.* New York: Lenox Club, 1917.

Ford, Paul L. *Franklin Bibliography: A List of Books Written by or Relating to Benjamin Franklin.* [1889]. Boston: Mitford House, 1972.

Franklin, Benjamin. *A Register and Index of his Papers in the Library of Congress.* Washington, D.C.: Library of Congress Manuscript Division, 1973.

Hayes, I.M., ed. *Calendar of the Papers of Benjamin Franklin in the Library of the American Philosophical Society.* Philadelphia: American Philosophical Society, 1908.

Lingelbach, William E. "Benjamin Franklin's Papers in the American Philosophical Society," *Proceedings.* American Philosophical Society 99(1955):359–380.

COLLECTED WORKS

Bigelow, John, ed. *The Complete Works of Benjamin Franklin.* 10 vols. New York: J.P. Putnam's Sons, 1887–1889.

Jorgenson, Chester E. and Frank L. Mott. *Benjamin Franklin: Representative Selections.* New York: Hill & Wang, 1962.

Labaree, Leonard and William B. Willcox, eds. *The Papers of Benjamin Franklin.* 21 vols. New Haven: Yale University Press, 1950–1978.

Sparks, Jared. *The Works of Benjamin Franklin.* 10 vols. Boston: Tappan & Whittemore, 1840.

Sullivan, James, *et. al. The Papers of Sir William Johnson.* 14 vols. Albany: University of the State of New York, 1921–1965.

PRIMARY SOURCES

Published Primary Sources

———. "Journal of the Proceedings Held at Albany in 1754." *Massachusetts Historical Society Collections* 3rd series, Vol. 5:5–74.

———. "Journal of the Treaty Held at Philadelphia in August, 1775, With the Six Nations by the Commissioners of the Twelve United Colonies." *Massachusetts Historical Society Collections* 3rd series, Vol. 5:75–100.

———. *Several Conferences Between . . . Quakers . . . and Deputies from the Six Nations.* New Castle Upon Tyne, Penn: I. Thompson & Co., 1756.

———. *An Account of Conferences Held and Treaties Made by Major General Sir William Johnson, Bart., and the Chief Sachems and Warriors of the Six Nations, etc.* London: A. Millar, 1756.

Atkinson, Theodore. "Accounts of the Albany Conference of 1754." Ed. by Beverly McAnear. *Mississippi Valley Historical Review* 39(1953):727–746.

Bartram, John. *Observations . . . Made in His Travels from Pensilvania to Onondaga, Oswego and the Lake Ontario.* London: no publisher, 1751.

———. *Observations on the Inhabitants . . . and Other Matters . . . Made by Mr. John Bartram, in His Travels from Pensilvania to Onondaga, Oswego and the Lake Ontario, in Canada.* London: no publisher, 1753.

Carver, Jonathan. *Travels Through the Interior Parts of North America With a Concise History . . . of the Indians.* London: no publisher, 1778.

———. *Three Years' Travels Through the Interior Parts of North America in the Years 1766, 1767 and 1768.* Philadelphia: Joseph Crukhart, 1792.

Douglass, William. *A Summary, Historical and Political, of the British Settlements in North America.* 2 vols. London: R.J. Dodsley, 1760.

Farrand, Max. *The Records of the Constitutional Convention of 1787.* 3 vols. New Haven: Yale University Press, 1911.

Hazard, Samuel, ed. *Pennsylvania Archives.* Philadelphia: Joseph Severns & Co., 1852.

Hopkins, Stephen A. *A True Representation of the Plan Formed at Albany in 1754 for Uniting all the British Northern Colonies.* Rhode Island Historical Tracts No. 9. Providence: Rhode Island Historical Society, 1880.

Hunter, John Dunn. *Memoirs of a Captivity Among the Indians of North America.* [1824]. New York: Schocken, 1973.

Kennedy, Archibald. *Serious Considerations on the Present State of the Affairs of the Northern Colonies.* New York: R. Griffiths, 1754.

———. *The Importance of Gaining and Preserving the Friendship of the Indians to the British Interest Considered.* New York: James Parker, 1751.

———. *Serious Advice to the Inhabitants of the Northern Colonies on the Present Situation of Affairs.* New York: A. Kennedy, 1755.

Marshe, Witham. *Journal of the Treaty Held With the Six Nations by the Commissioners of Maryland and Other Provinces at Lancaster in 1744.* Massachusetts Historical Society Collections 1800. Vol. 7:171–201. Boston: Massachusetts Historical Society, 1801.

O'Callaghan, E.B., ed., *Documentary History of the State of New York.* Albany: Weed, Parsons & Co., 1849. Volume 1.

———. *Documents Relative to the Colonial History of New York.* Albany: Weed, Parsons & Co., 1855. Volume 6.

Pennsylvania, State of. *Minutes of the Provincial Council of Pennsylvania.* Philadelphia: Joseph Severns & Co., 1852.

Pownall, Thomas. *Considerations Toward a General Plan of Measures for the English Provinces.* New York: Parker & Weyman, 1756.

———. *The Administration of the Colonies.* 4th ed. London: J. Walter, 1768.

Tilghman, Tench. *Memoir of Lt. Col. Tench Tilghman.* [1876]. New York: Arno Press, 1971.

Van Doren, Carl and Julian P. Boyd, eds. *Indian Treaties Printed by Benjamin Franklin.* Philadelphia: Pennsylvania Historical Society, 1938.

Van Doren, Carl. *Letters and Papers of Benjamin Franklin and Richard Jackson.* Philadelphia: American Philosophical Society, 1947.

————. *Benjamin Franklin's Autobiographical Writings.* New York: The Viking Press, 1945.

Wraxall, Peter. *An Abridgement of the Indian Affairs . . . 1678–1751.* Ed. by Charles H. McIlwain. Cambridge: Harvard University Press, 1915.

Unpublished Primary Sources

————. *Account of a Meeting of the Commissioners of Indian Affairs, August 9, 1745.* American Philosophical Society.

Atkinson, Theodore. *Memo Book of My Journey as One of the Commissioners to the Six Nations, 1754.* Manuscript Division, Library of Congress.

Croghan, George. "Journal—April 3 to November 18, 1759." American Philosophical Society.

————. "Journal Relating to a Meeting With the Indians." American Philosophical Society.

Franklin, Benjamin. "Remarks on the Plan for Regulating the Indian Trade 1765–1766." Library of Congress.

————. "Memorandum of a Conference With the Indians at Carlisle, September 26, 1753." American Philosophical Society..

————. "Talk to the Old Chief." [June 30, 1787]. Library of Congress, Manuscript Division.

————. "To the Beloved Woman." [June 30, 1787]. Library of Congress, Manuscript Division.

————. "To Gov. Sevier, from Philadelphia." [June 30, 1787]. Library of Congress, Manuscript Division.

————. "To the Cornstalk, Cherokee." [June 30, 1787]. Library of Congress, Manuscript Division.

————. "To Count de Buffon." [November 19, 1787]. Library of Congress, Manuscript Division.

Horsfield, Timothy. [1708–1773, Justice of the Peace, Bethlehem, Pa.] *Papers, 1733–1771.* 2 vols. American Philosophical Society.

Library of Congress. Colonial Office Records, Group 5. Indian Treaties 1748–1763.

————. Public Records Office (War office) Collections 34, 38, 39. Sir William Johnson Papers.

Misc. Manuscripts on Indian Affairs 1737–1775. 5 vols. American Philosophical Society.

Wallace, Paul A.W. *Benjamin Franklin's Fingerprints.* [1953]. American Philosophical Society.

Weiser, Conrad. "Letter to James Logan." [October 15, 1747]. American Philosophical Society.

SECONDARY SOURCES

Published Secondary Sources

ARTICLES AND SHORT MONOGRAPHS

Aldridge, Alfred O. "Franklin's Letter on Indians and Germans." *Proceedings.* American Philosophical Society 90:4(1947):391–395.

————. "Franklin's Deistical Indians." *Proceedings.* American Philosophical Society 90:4(1947):398–410.

Bibliography

Becker, Carl. "Benjamin Franklin." *Dictionary of American Biography.* New York: Charles Scribner's Sons, 1931 6:585–598.

Billington, R.A. "The Fort Stanwix Treaty of 1768." *New York History* 25(1944):182–194.

Eddy, George S. "The Franklin Library." *Proceedings.* American Antiquarian Society 34(1924):208–226.

Gipson, Lawrence H. "Thomas Hutchinson and the Framing of the Albany Plan of Union of 1754." *Pennsylvania Magazine of History and Biography* (1950):5–35.

———. "The Drafting of the Albany Plan of Union: A Problem in Semantics." *Pennsylvania History* 26(1959):290–316.

Hallowell, A. Irving. "The Backwash of the Frontier: The Impact of the Indian on American Culture." Edited by Walker D. Lyman and Clifton B. Kroeber. *The Frontier in Perspective.* Madison: University of Wisconsin Press, 1957.

Hamilton, Milton W. "Myths and Legends of Sir William Johnson." *New York History* 34(1953):3–26.

McLaughlin, Andrew C. "The Background of American Federalism." *American Political Science Review* 12(1918):215–240.

Matthews, Lois K. "Benjamin Franklin's Plans for a Colonial Union." *American Political Science Review* 8(1914):393–412.

Olson, Alson G. "The British Government and Colonial Union 1754." *William and Mary Quarterly* 3rd series 17(1960):22–23.

Ranney, John C. "The Bases of American Federalism." *William and Mary Quarterly* 3rd series 3(1946):1–35.

BOOKS AND LONGER MONOGRAPHS

Aldridge, Alfred O. *Benjamin Franklin and Nature's God.* Durham, N.C.: Duke University Press, 1967.

———. *Benjamin Franklin: Philosopher and Man.* Philadelphia: J. B. Lippincott, 1965.

Beauchamp, William M. *The Life of Conrad Weiser.* Syracuse: Onondaga County Historical Association, 1925.

Brewster, William. *The Pennsylvania and New York Frontier 1720 to 1783.* Philadelphia: George S. MacManus Co., 1954.

Buell, Augustus C. *Sir William Johnson.* New York: Appleton & Co., 1903.

Conner, Paul W. *Poor Richard's Politicks: Benjamin Franklin and the New American Order.* New York: Oxford University Press, 1965.

Crane, Verner W. *Benjamin Franklin: Englishman and American.* Providence, R.I.: Brown University, 1936.

———. *Benjamin Franklin and a Rising People.* Edited by Oscar Handlin. Boston: Little, Brown & Co., 1954.

———. *Benjamin Franklin's Letters to the Press.* Chapel Hill: University of North Carolina Press, 1950.

Eckert, Allan W. *Wilderness Empire: A Narrative.* Boston: Little, Brown & Co., 1969.

Eiselen, Malcolm R. *Franklin's Political Theories.* Garden City, N.Y.: Doubleday, Doran & Co., 1928.

Fox, Edith M. *Land Speculation in the Mohawk County.* Ithaca, N.Y.: Cornell University Press, 1949.

Flexner, James T. *Mohawk Baronet: Sir William Johnson of New York.* New York: Harper & Bros., 1959.

Gipson, Lawrence H. *Zones of International Friction: The Great Lakes Frontier, Canada, India 1748–1754*. New York: Alfred A. Knopf, 1942.

Gooch, George P. *The History of English Democratic Ideas in the Seventeenth Century*. Cambridge, England: The University Press, 1898.

Graeff, Arthur D. *Conrad Weiser: Pennsylvania Peacemaker*. Allentown, Pa.: German Folklore Society, no date.

Griffis, William E. *Sir William Johnson and the Six Nations*. New York: Dodd, Mead & Co., 1891.

Hamilton, Milton W. *Sir William Johnson: Colonial American 1715–1763*. Port Washington, N.Y.: Kennikat Press, 1976.

Henry, Thomas R. *Wilderness Messiah: The Story of Hiawatha and the Iroquois*. New York: Bonanza Books, 1955.

Howe, John R., ed. *The Role of Ideology in the American Revolution*. New York: Holt, Rinehart, Winston, 1970.

Huntington, Ellsworth. *The Red Man's Continent: A Chronicle of Aboriginal America*. New Haven: Yale University Press, 1921.

Jacobs, Wilbur. *Wilderness Politics and Indian Gifts: The Northern Colonial Frontier 1748–1763*. Lincoln: University of Nebraska Press, 1950.

Judd, Jacob and Irwin Polisbook, eds. *Aspects of Early New York Society and Politics*. Tarrytown, N.Y.: Sleepy Hollow Restoration, 1974.

Ketcham, Ralph L., ed. *The Political Thought of Benjamin Franklin*. New York: Bobbs-Merrill, 1965.

Keys, Alice M. *Cadwallader Colden: A Representative Eighteenth Century Official*. New York: Columbia University Press, 1906.

Kraus, Michael. *The Atlantic Civilization: Eighteenth Century Origins*. New York: Russell & Russell, 1949.

Leach, Douglas E. *The Northern Colonial Frontier 1607–1763*. New York: Holt, Rinehart, Winston 1966.

Merritt, Richard L. *Symbols of American Community 1735–1775*. New Haven: Yale University Press, 1966.

Newbold, Robert C. *The Albany Congress and Plan of Union of 1754*. New York: Vantage Press, 1955.

Osgood, Herbert L. *The American Colonies in the Eighteenth Century*. Gloucester, Mass.: Peter Smith, 1958.

Pearce, Roy Harvey. *The Savages of America: A Study of the Indian and the Idea of Civilization*. Baltimore: Johns Hopkins University Press, 1965.

Pound, Arthur. *Johnson of the Mohawks*. New York: Macmillan, 1930.

Richter, Conrad. *The Light in the Forest*. New York: Alfred A. Knopf, 1953.

Sanford, Charles L., ed. *Benjamin Franklin and the American Character*. Boston: D. C. Heath Co., 1955.

Savelle, Max. *Seeds of Liberty: The Genesis of the American Mind*. New York: Alfred A. Knopf, 1948.

———. *The Diplomatic History of the Canadian Boundary 1749–1763*. New Haven: Yale University Press, 1940.

———. *Empires to Nations: Expansion in America 1713–1824*. Minneapolis: University of Minnesota Press, 1974.

Seymour, Flora W. *Lords of the Valley: Sir William Johnson and His Mohawk Brothers*. New York: Longman, Green & Co., 1930.

Stourzh, Gerald. *Benjamin Franklin and American Foreign Policy*. [1954] Chicago: University of Chicago Press, 1969.

Bibliography

Thwaites, Reuben G. *Early Western Travels 1748–1846.* Cleveland: Arthur H. Clarke, 1904. Vol. 1.

Van Doren, Carl. *Benjamin Franklin.* New York: The Viking Press, 1938.

Volwiler, Albert T. *George Croghan and the Western Movement 1741–1782.* Cleveland: Arthur H. Clark Co., 1926.

Wainwright, Nicholas B. *George Croghan: Wilderness Diplomat.* Chapel Hill: University of North Carolina Press, 1959.

Wallace, Paul A. W. *Conrad Weiser: Friend of Colonist and Mahowk.* Philadelphia: University of Pennsylvania Press, 1945.

Walton, Joseph S. *Conrad Weiser and the Indian Policy of Pennsylvania.* Philadelphia: George H. Jacobs Co., 1900.

Ward, Harry M. *Unite or Die: Intercolony Relations 1690–1763.* Port Washington, N.Y.: Kennikat Press, 1971.

Zolla, Elemire. *The Writer and the Shaman: A Morphology of the American Indian.* New York: Harcourt, Brace, Jovanovich.

Unpublished Secondary Sources

THESES AND DISSERTATIONS

Bain, Florence D. *The Political Theory of Benjamin Franklin.* M.A. thesis, University of Washington, 1927.

Gatke, Robert M. *Plans of American Colonial Union 1643–1754.* Ph.D. dissertation, American University, 1925.

Graeff, Arthur D. *Conrad Weiser—Interpreter.* M.A. thesis, Temple University, 1932.

Maggs, Helen L. *Sir William Johnson's Role in the French and Indian War.* M.A. thesis, Syracuse University, 1942.

Mathur, Mary E. *The Iroquois in Time and Space: A Native American Nationalistic Movement.* Ph.D. dissertation, University of Wisconsin, 1971.

Miles, Richard D. *The Political Philosophy of Benjamin Franklin.* Ph.D. dissertation, University of Michigan, 1948.

Morais, Herbert M. *Deism in Eighteenth Century America.* Ph.D. dissertation, Columbia University, 1934.

Thomas Jefferson

FINDING AIDS

Hill, Edward E., ed. *Preliminary Inventory of the Records of the Bureau of Indian Affairs.* Washington, D.C.: National Archives, 1965.

Michigan, University of. William L. Clements Library. *Thomas Jefferson: 1743–1943; A Guide to Rare Books, Maps and Manuscripts Exhibited at the University of Michigan.* Ann Arbor, Mich.: William L. Clements Library, 1943.

National Archives. *Documents Relating to the Negotiation of Ratified and Unratified Treaties With Various Indian Tribes 1801–1869.* Washington, D.C.: National Archives, 1965.

———. *Letters Received by the Secretary of War Relating to Indian Affairs 1800–1823*. Washington, D.C.: National Archives, 1965.

———. *Letters Sent by the Secretary of War Relating to Indian Affairs 1800–1824*. Washington, D.C.: National Archives, 1965.

———. *Misc. Letters Sent by the General Land Office 1796–1889*. Washington, D.C.: National Archives, 1965.

———. *Papers of the Continental Congress 1774–1789*. Washington, D.C.: National Archives, 1965.

———. *Special Files of the Office of Indian Affairs 1807–1904*. Washington, D.C.: National Archives, 1965.

Thurlow, Constance E. and Francis L. Berkeley, eds. *The Jefferson Papers of the University of Virginia*. Charlottesville, Va.: University of Virginia Library, 1950.

United States of America. Department of State. *Calendar of the Correspondence of Thomas Jefferson*. 2 vols. Washington, D.C.: Department of State, 1895.

Virginia, University of. *Guide to the Manuscript Edition of the Jefferson Papers of the University of Virginia 1732–1828*. Charlottesville, Va.: University of Virginia, 1977.

COLLECTED WORKS

Boyd, Julian P., ed. *The Papers of Thomas Jefferson*. Princeton, N.J.: Princeton University Press, 1950–1974.

Ford, Paul L., ed. *The Writings of Thomas Jefferson*. New York: J. P. Putnam's Sons, 1892–1899.

Lipscomb, Andrew A. and Albert E. Bergh, eds. *The Writings of Thomas Jefferson*. Washington, D.C.: Jefferson Memorial Associates, 1903.

Washington, H.A., ed. *The Writings of Thomas Jefferson*. 9 vols. New York: John C. Riker, 1853–1854.

PRIMARY SOURCES

Published Primary Sources

———. *A Series of Answers to Certain Popular Objections Against Separating from the Rebellious Colonies. Being The Concluding Tract of the Dean of Gloucester on the Subject of American Affairs*. Gloucester, England: R. Raikes, 1776.

Black, Nancy B. and Bette S. Weidman. *White on Red: Images of the American Indian*. Port Washington, N.Y.: Kennikat Press, 1976.

Bland, Richard. *An Inquiry into the Rights of the British Colonies*. Williamsburg, Va.: Appeals Press, 1776.

Cherokee Nation. *Constitution and Laws of the Cherokee Nation*. Tahlequah, Cherokee Nation: Cherokee Nation Printers, 1852.

Chinard, Gilbert, ed. *The Literary Bible of Thomas Jefferson*. Baltimore: Johns Hopkins University Press, 1928.

———. *The Correspondence of Thomas Jefferson and du Pont de Nemours*. Baltimore: Johns Hopkins University Presss, 1931.

———. *The Commonplace Book of Thomas Jefferson: A Repository of his Ideas on Government*. Baltimore: Johns Hopkins University Press, 1926.

Bibliography

Council on Interracial Books for Children. *Chronicles of American Indian Protest.* New York: Council on Interracial Books for Children, 1979.

Foner, Philip S. *The Basic Writings of Thomas Jefferson.* New York: Willey Book Company, 1944.

Forbes, Jack B. *The Indian in America's Past.* Englewood Cliffs, N.J.: Prentice Hall, 1964.

Ford, Worthington C. *Some Jefferson Correspondence 1775–1787.* Boston: David Clapp & Son, 1902.

Library of Congress. *Some Papers Laid Before the Continental Congress 1776, Taken from Volumes 4 Through 6 of the Journals of the Continental Congress Issued by the Library of Congress.* Washington, D.C.: Government Printing Office, 1905.

Mullet, Charles F., ed. "Some Political Writings of James Otis." *University of Missouri Studies* 4 July and October, 1929.

Padover, Saul K. *Thomas Jefferson on Democracy.* New York: Appleton-Century Co., 1939.

Sowerby, E. Millicent, ed. *Catalogue of the Library of Thomas Jefferson.* 5 vols. Washington, D.C.: Library of Congress, 1952–1959.

Vogel, Virgil J. *This Country Was Ours: Documentary History of the American Indian.* New York: Harper & Row, 1972.

Washburn, Wilcomb. *The Indian and the White Man.* New York: University Press, 1964.

Unpublished Primary Sources

Jefferson, Thomas. "To the Brothers of the Delaware and Shawnee Nations." [Feb. 10, 1801]. Manuscript Division, Library of Congress.

———. "To the Chiefs of the Cherokee Nation." [November 24, 1792]. Manuscript Division, Library of Congress.

———. "To the Chiefs of the Choctaw Nation." [March 13, 1805]. Manuscript Division, Library of Congress.

———. "To the Chiefs of the Creek Nation." [Nov. 1, 1805]. Manuscript Division, Library of Congress.

———. "To the Chiefs of the Shawnees." [Jan 10, 1809]. Manuscript Division, Library of Congress.

———. "To Chickasaw Nation." [March 7, 1805]. Manuscript Division, Library of Congress.

———. "To Choctaw Indians." [Dec. 13, 1807]. Manuscript Division, Library of Congress.

———. "To Choctaw Nation." [Dec. 17, 1807]. Manuscript Division, Library of Congress.

———. "Contents of an Act Concerning Intercourse With the Indian Tribes." [Jan. 13, 1793]. Manuscript Division, Library of Congress.

———. "To Cornplanter." [Feb. 11, 1803]. Manuscript Division, Library of Congress.

———. "To Deputies of the Cherokees." [Jan. 9, 1809]. Manuscript Division, Library of Congress.

———. "Extract From a Speech by the Commissioners of the United States to the Chiefs of the Cherokees at Southwest Point." [Sept. 4, 1801]. Manuscript Division, Library of Congress.

————. "To Handsome Lake." [Feb. 12, 1803]. Manuscript Division, Library of Congress.

————. "To Indian Affairs Commissioners." [Sept. 16, 1801]. Manuscript Division, Library of Congress.

————. "To My Children, Chiefs of the Upper Cherokees." [May 4, 1808]. Manuscript Division, Library of Congress.

————. "To My Friends and Children, Chiefs of the Foxes, Sacs. . . ." [No date]. Manuscript Division, Library of Congress.

————. "To My Friends and Children, Chiefs of the Cherokee Nation." [Jan. 10, 1806]. Manuscript Division, Library of Congress.

————. "Report of the Secretary of State on Chickasaw and Cherokee Lands." [Feb. 16, 1793]. Manuscript Division, Library of Congress.

————. "To Shawnee Indian Nation." [Feb. 19, 1807]. Manuscript Division, Library of Congress.

————. "A Short Narration of My Last Journey to the Western Country." [1792]. Manuscript Division, Library of Congress.

SECONDARY SOURCES

Published Secondary Sources

ARTICLES AND SHORT MONOGRAPHS

Bailyn, Bernard. "Political Experience and Enlightenment Ideas in Eighteenth Century America." *American Historical Review* 62(1962):339–351.

Conway, Moncure D. *The Life of Thomas Paine*. 2 vols. New York: J.P. Putnam's Sons, 1908.

Dorfman, Joseph. "The Economic Philosophy of Thomas Jefferson." *Political Science Quarterly* 55(1940):98–121.

Dumbauld, Edward. *The Declaration of Independence and What it Means Today*. Norman: University of Oklahoma Press, 1950.

Eckert, Allan W. *Wilderness Empire: A Narrative*. Boston: Little, Brown & Co., 1969.

Edwards, Samuel, *REBEL: A Biography of Tom Paine*. New York: Praeger, 1974.

Ganter, Herbert L. "Jefferson's Pursuit of Happiness and Some Forgotten Men." 3rd series 16(July, 1936):422–434; Part 2: 3rd series 16(October, 1936): 558–585.

Gipson, Lawrence H. *The Coming of the Revolution 1763–1775*. New York: Harper & Bros., 1954.

Graymont, Barbara. *The Iroquois in the American Revolution*. Syracuse: Syracuse University Press, 1972.

Grinde, Donald A., Jr. *The Iroquois and the Founding of the American Nation*. San Francisco: Indian Historian Press, 1977.

Hagan, William T. *Longhouse Diplomacy and Frontier Warfare: The Iroquois Confederacy in the American Revolution*. Albany: New York State American Revolution Bicentennial Commission, 1976.

Harmon, George D. *Sixty Years of Indian Affairs 1789–1850*. Chapel Hill: University of North Carolina Press, 1941.

Hawke, David F. *Paine*. New York: Harper & Row, 1974.

Howe, John R., Jr. *The Role of Ideology in the American Revolution*. New York: Holt, Rinehart, Winston, 1970.

Bibliography

Huntington, Ellsworth. *The Red Man's Continent: A Chronicle of Aboriginal America.* New Haven: Yale University Press, 1921.

Jacob, John J. "A Biographical Sketch of Captain Michael Cresap." Parsons, W. Va.: McClain Printing Co., 1971.

Jefferson, Thomas. "Shickellamy and His Son Logan." American Scenic and Historical Preservation Society 21st *Annual Report.* [1916]. Appendix D: 599–611.

Jensen, Merrill. *The Articles of Confederation: An Interpretation of the Social Constitutional History of the American Revolution, 1774–1781.* Madison: University of Wisconsin Press, 1940.

Kimball, Marie. *Jefferson: The Road to Glory.* New York: Coward-McCann, 1943.

Persinger, C.E. "The Political Philosophy of Thomas Paine." University of Nebraska *Graduate Bulletin C.* Series 6(1901):54–74.

Red Jacket. "A Long-Lost Speech of Red Jacket." Edited by John W. Sanborn. Friendship, N.W.: J. W. Sanborn, 1912.

———. *Jefferson, Nationalism and the Enlightenment.* New York: George Braziller, 1975.

Steele, Oliver G. "Red Jacket and His Portrait." *Publications of the Buffalo Historical Society* 2(1880):216–226.

Sullivan, James. "The Antecedents of the Declaration of Independence." American Historical Association *Annual Report.* [1902]. Washington, D.C.: Government Printing Office, 1903.

BOOKS AND LONGER MONOGRAPHS

Beard, Charles A. *Economic Origins of Jeffersonian Democracy.* New York: Macmillan, 1927.

Becker, Carl. *The Declaration of Independence: A Study in the History of Political Ideas.* New York: Peter Smith, 1940.

Berkhofer, Robert F. *The White Man's Indian: Images of the American Indian from Columbus to the Present.* New York: Alfred A. Knopf, 1978.

Bowers, Claude G. *The Young Jefferson 1743–1789.* Cambridge, Mass.: Houghton-Mifflin, 1945.

Boyd, Julian P. *The Declaration of Independence: Evolution of the Text. . . .* Washington, D.C.: Library of Congress. 1943.

Brodie, Fawn M. *Thomas Jefferson: An Intimate History.* New York: W. W. Norton, 1974.

Brown, John P. *Old Frontier: Story of the Cherokee Indians from Earliest Times to the Date of Their Removal in 1838.* Kingsport, Tenn.: Southern Publishing, 1938.

Chinard, Gilbert. *Thomas Jefferson: The Apostle of Americanism.* Boston: Little, Brown & Co., 1939.

Colbourn, H. Trevor. *The Lamp of Experience: Whig History and the Intellectual Origins of the American Revolution.* Chapel Hill: University of North Carolina Press, 1965.

Commager, Henry S. *The Empire of Reason: How Europe Imagined and America Realized the Enlightenment.* Garden City, N.Y.: Doubleday, 1977.

Jones, Howard. *Tah-jah-jute, or Logan, the Mingo Chief. . . .* Circleville, Ohio: No publisher, 1937.

Koch, Adrienne. *The American Enlightenment: The Shaping of the American Experiment and a Free Society.* New York: George Braziller, 1965.

———. *Power, Morals and the Founding Fathers: Essays in the Interpretation of the American Enlightenment.* Ithaca, N.Y.: Cornell University Press, 1961.

———., and William Peden, eds. *The Life and Selected Writings of Thomas Jefferson.* New York: The Modern Library/Random House, 1944.

———. *The Philosophy of Thomas Jefferson.* Gloucester, Mass.: Peter Smith, 1957.

Lynd, Staughton. *The Intellectual Origins of American Radicalism.* New York: Pantheon, 1968.

McIlwain, Charles H. *The American Revolution: A Constitutional Interpretation.* New York: Macmillan, 1924.

Malone, Dumas. *Jefferson and his Time.* 4 vols. Boston: Little, Brown & Co., 1948–1974.

May, Henry F. *The Enlightenment in America.* New York: Oxford University Press, 1976.

Milling, Chapman J. *Red Carolinians.* Chapel Hill: University of North Carolina Press, 1940.

Morgan, Edmund S. *The Birth of the Republic 1763–1789.* Chicago: University of Chicago Press, 1956.

Mullet, Charles F. *Fundamental Law and the American Revolution 1760–1776.* New York: Octagon Books, 1966.

Palmer, R. R. *The Age of Democratic Revolution: A Political History of Europe and America.* Princeton, N.J.: Princeton University Press, 1959.

Pearce, Roy H. *the Savages of America: A Study of the Indian and the Idea of Civilization.* Baltimore: John Hopkins University Press, 1965.

Ritchie, David G. *Natural Rights: A Criticism of Some Political and Ethical Conceptions.* New York: Macmillan, 1895.

Rossiter, Clinton. *The Political Thought of the American Revolution.* New York: Harcourt, Brace, World, 1953.

Royce, Charles C. *The Cherokee Nation of Indians.* Chicago: Aldine Publishing Co., 1975.

Sanford, Charles. *The Quest for Paradise: Europe and the American Moral Imagination.* Urbana: University of Illinois Press, 1961.

Sheehan, Bernhard. *Seeds of Extinction: Jeffersonian Philanthropy and the American Indian.* Chapel Hill: University of North Carolina Press, 1973.

Skeen, Carl E. *Jefferson and the West 1798–1808.* Columbus, Ohio: Ohio State Museum, 1960.

Straus, Oscar S. *The Origins of the Republican Form of Government in the United States.* New York: Houghton-Mifflin, 1911.

Van Doren, Carl. *The Story of the Making and Ratifying of the Constitution of the United States.* New York: The Viking Press, 1948.

Wain, John, ed. *An Edmund Wilson Celebration.* Oxford, England: Phaidon Press Ltd., 1978.

Washburn, Wilcomb E. *The Indian in America.* New York: Harper & Row, 1975.

Watson, Thomas E. *The Life and Times of Thomas Jefferson.* New York: D. Appleton & Co., 1908.

Wills, Gary. *Inventing America: Jefferson's Declaration of Independence.* Garden City, N.Y.: Doubleday, 1978.

Wiltse, Charles M. *The Jeffersonian Tradition in American Democracy.* Chapel Hill: University of North Carolina Press, 1935.

Bibliography

Wright, Benjamin F. *American Interpretations of Natural Law: A Study in the History of Political Thought.* Cambridge: Harvard University Press, 1931.
Wright, Edmond, ed. *Causes and Consequences of the American Revolution.* Chicago: Quadrangle Books, 1966.
Zolla, Elemire. *The Writer and the Shaman: A Morphology of the American Indian.* New York: Harcourt, Brace, Jovanovich, 1973.

Unpublished Secondary Sources
THESES AND DISSERTATIONS
Dai, Shen Yu. *The Democratic Philosophies of Thomas Jefferson and Mencius.* M.A. thesis, University of Washington, 1949.
Hatch, Ethel S. *Tom Paine's Contribution to Democracy.* M.A. thesis, University of Washington, 1918.
King, Arnold K. *Thomas Paine in America 1774–1787.* Ph.D. dissertation, University of Chicago, 1951.
Morais, Herbert M. *Deism in Eighteenth Century America.* Ph.D. dissertation, Columbia University, 1934.

Afterword

Barnett, H. G. *Innovation: The Basis of Cultural Change.* New York: McGraw-Hill, 1953.
Berkhofer, Robert F., Jr. *The White Man's Indian: Images of the American Indian from Columbus to the Present.* New York: Alfred A. Knopf, 1978.
Brodie, Fawn M. *Thomas Jefferson: An Intimate History.* New York: W. W. Norton & Co., 1974.
Bryson, Lyman. *The Communication of Ideas.* New York: Harper & Bros., 1948.
Engels, Frederich. "The Origin of the Family, Private Property and the State." Marx and Engels, *Selected Works.* New York: International Publishers, 1968.
Gipson, Lawrence H. *The Coming of the Revolution 1763–1775.* New York: Harper & Bros., 1954.
Hallowell, A. Irving. "The Backwash of the Frontier: The Impact of the American Indian on American Culture." Edited by Walker D. Wyman and Clifton B. Kroeber. *The Frontier in Perspective.* Madison: University of Wisconsin Press, 1957.
Koch, Adrienne. *The American Enlightenment: The Shaping of the American Experiment and a Free Society.* New York: George Braziller, 1965.
———. *The Philosophy of Thomas Jefferson.* Gloucester, Mass.: Peter Smith, 1957.
Kraus, Michael. *The Atlantic Civilization: Eighteenth Century Origins.* New York: Russell & Russell, 1949.
Lynd, Staughton. *The Intellectual Origins of American Radicalism.* New York: Pantheon, 1968.
Morgan, Lewis Henry. *Ancient Society.* New York: Henry Holt, 1877.
Mullet, Charles F. *Fundamental Law and the American Revolution 1760–1776.* New York: Octagon Books, 1966.

Afterword

Palmer, R.R. *The Age of Democratic Revolution: A Political History of Europe and America 1760–1800.* Princeton: Princeton University Press, 1959.

Pearce, Roy H. *The Savages of America: A Study of the Indian and the Idea of Civilization.* Baltimore: Johns Hopkins University Press, 1965.

Prosser, Michael H., ed. *Intercommunication Among Nations and Peoples.* New York: Harper and Row, 1973.

Rabinowitz, Richard. "At Jefferson's Feet." *The Nation,* March 31, 1979 pp. 342–344.

Sanford, Charles. *The Quest for Paradise: Europe and the American Moral Imagination.* Urbana: University of Illinois Press, 1961.

Sullivan, James. "The Antecedents of the Declaration of Independence." *American Historical Association Annual Report.* [1902]. 2 vols. Washington, D.C.: Government Printing Office, (1903)1:65–86.

Turner, Frederick J. *The Frontier in American History.* [1920]. New York: Henry Holt & Co., 1947.

Wallace, Paul A. W. *Conrad Weiser: Friend of Colonist and Mohawk.* Philadelphia: University of Pennsylvania Press, 1945.

Wright, Benjamin F. *American Interpretations of Natural Law: A Study in the History of Political Thought.* Cambridge: Harvard University Press, 1931.

Zikmund, Joseph. *The Peloponnesian League and the Iroquois Confederacy: A Comparative Study of Two Interstate Organizations.* Ph.D. dissertation, Chicago University, 1950.

I N D E X

of names cited in the

B I B L I O G R A P H Y

INDEX

ADAIR, James
History of the American Indians
(1775), quoted, 40.
ADAMS, John
Mentioned, 15. Refuses Jefferson's request to write Declaration of Independence, 100. Admires Thomas Jefferson's "masterly pen," 100. Edits Thomas Jefferson's declaration, 100.
AKWESASNE NOTES (Mohawk journal)
Publisher of Great Law of Peace, 21, 23.
ALBANY, New York
As frontier outpost, 42, 69. As frequent site of treaty councils, 53. Courthouse, 69, Dutch architecture in, 69. Canassatego visits, 90.
ALBANY CONGRESS, ALBANY PLAN OF UNION
65. Franklin on Archibald Kennedy at, 65. Iroquois' issues at, 68. Benjamin Franklin represents Pennsylvania at. Proceedings, 69–76. Purposes of meeting, 69. Approval of Benjamin Franklin's plan of union, 70, 72. Debate on Albany plan, 70–71. Provisions of Albany plan 71–73. Similar to Iroquois system, 72. Rejected by Colonial Assemblies, 74. As basis for Benjamin Franklin's Articles of Confederation, 75.
ALDRIDGE, ALFRED O.
On Benjamin Franklin and Deism, 89.
ALEXANDER, James
And Albany plan, 70.

AMERICAN PHILOSOPHICAL SOCIETY
Benjamin Franklin and, 64.
AMERICAN REVOLUTION
Mentioned, xvi, 34, 54.
Role of Iroquois thought in, 14–15. Indian battle tactics in, 37.
Upper classes flee, 110.
Natural rights and, 115.
ANGLES, 106.
ANGLO-SAXONS
Jefferson, natural rights of, 115.
ARMSTRONG, John (Indian trader)
Murdered by Delawares, 61.
ATOTARHO (Office of chief sachem, Iroquois Confederacy), 22, 25.

BERKHOFER, Robert F.
Quotes John Locke, 120.
BRITAIN, BRITISH (*See also:* England, English)
Mentioned, 34, 35.
"Cold war" with France, 44–45.
Source of immigration, 34.
Trade with Iroquois, Lancaster treaty (1744), 46, 47.
Motivations of trade, gifts, 47.
Rivalry with France, 59.
Iroquois deny King's authority, 62.
War with France, 66.
Parliament compared to Indian councils, 74.
Rejects Albany plan, 74.
Spies watch Benjamin Franklin, 74.
Taxes inflame colonists, 75.
Evict French from North America (1763), 77.
Agents cut gift-giving, 78.
Separation of America from, 97.

[155]

Index

COHEN, Felix
"Americanizing the White Man,"
3, 7, 13, 14–15.
Indians' democratic traditions, 13.
Role of women, Indian cultures, 13,
19.
Indian governments' federalism,
13–14.
COLDEN, Rev. Alexander
Father of Cadwallader Colden, 36.
COLDEN, Cadwallader
"Indians have outdone the
Romans," xiv, 36–37, 39, 41, 84.
Iroquois and liberty, 33.
On Iroquois sociopolitical system,
36.
Sketch of life, 36.
Indians as "living images" of Euro-
pean ancestors, 37.
Iroquois and use of public opinion,
38, 112.
Mentioned, 121.
Iroquois and political liberty, 40.
Need for alliance with Iroquois, 41,
42, 67.
Importance of fur trade, 43.
Political purposes of trade with In-
dians, 44–45.
Participant in treaty councils, 47.
Relations with William Johnson,
51.
As Deist, 89.
Correspondence with Benjamin
Franklin: Colonial union, 62–63.
And Albany plan, 69.
Urges regulation of Indian trade, 73.
COLLINSON, Peter
Letter from Benjamin Franklin,
92–93.
COLUMBUS, Christopher
Mentioned, 3, 13.
Voyage narratives, 35.
COMMAGER, Henry Steele
Cited, xvi, 8f.
On state of nature and happiness,
112.
On Enlightenment thought, 120.
CONCORD, Massachusetts
Battle of (1775), 75, 99.
CONTINENTAL CONGRESS
Mentioned, 75.

And Declaration of Independence,
98–100.
Jefferson requested to author decla-
ration, 100.
Jefferson's reputation at, 100.
Conestoga manor, Pennsylvania,
CONESTOGA INDIANS
Indians attacked at (1763), 79.
Indians attacked at Lancaster, 79.
Remnant of Iroquois, 80.
Massacre described by Benjamin
Franklin, 80.
CONSTITUTION, United States
Mentioned, 15, 17, 18.
Benjamin Franklin on, 105.
CONSTITUTIONAL CONVEN-
TION, United States
Benjamin Franklin at, 72.
CONSTITUTION, Virginia
Jefferson and, 100.
CROGHAN, George
Land interests, Ohio Valley, 107f.
CUSTER BATTLE, 121.

DECLARATION OF INDEPEN-
DENCE
Posted in Philadelphia, 98.
Jefferson authors, 110, 111.
Ideas in, 102, 108, 117.
And right of revolution, 118.
DEER PIGEON (Iroquois Clan), 28.
DEISM
And Cadwallader Colden, 62.
And Benjamin Franklin, 62–63, 89.
Description of, 89.
As "natural religion," 89–90.
And universal moral sense, 89.
And Indian thought, 92.
DEGANWIDAH (Founder of Iro-
quois Confederacy), 12, 22, 26.
DELAWARE INDIANS
Murder of John Armstrong, Indian
trader, 61.
DOBYNS, Henry
Estimates of Indian populations,
124.
DONEGAL, Pennsylvania
Vigilantes attack Indians (1763),
79.
DONGAN, New York governor
On Iroquois military prowess, 45.

Index

Index

Index

Index

Index

Described (1763), 77–78.
Rumors of attack by "Paxton Men," 79, 80.
Described, mid 1770s, 98.
As "Grand Council fire" of Confederacy, 98.

PILGRIMS
Met by Squanto (1620), 4.
PILANT, Richard, 17.
PITTSBURGH, 34.
PLOG, Fred
Cited, 6.
PONTIAC
Opposes squatters, 78.
de la POTERIE, Monsieur
On Iroquois, 39.
POUND, Arthur
Cited, 11.
POWNALL, Thomas
Opposes confiscation of Indian land, 106.
PRESQUE ISLE
French fort at, 67.
PROVINCE ISLAND, Philadelphia
Indian settlement at, 79.
Rumors of attack: "Paxton Men," 79.
PURITANS, PURITANISM
Benjamin Franklin's distaste for orthodoxy of, 56.

QUAKERS
Tension with Frontier settlers, 79.
Form militia versus "Paxton Men," 81.
In Philadelphia, 98.

REAMAN, Elmore
Cited, 17.
REYNOLDS, Wynn R.
Examines Iroquois oratory, 41.
ROMAN REPUBLIC
Liberties in, 117.
ROMANS
Studies by Benjamin Franklin, Jefferson, et. al., 115.
ROSSITER, Clinton
On Benjamin Franklin and federalism, 73.

ROUSSEAU, Jean Jacques
Mentioned, xiv, 14, 120.
Ignites French imagination, 121.

SANFORD, Charles
Cited, 14, 16, 120.
American imagined as Garden of Eden, 115.
SAVELLE, Max
Cited, 5.
SAXONS, 106
SCARROOYADY
At Carlisle treaty council (1753), 68.
Urges regulation of Indian trade, 68.
Traders use of liquor: fraud, 68.
SCOTCH–IRISH
Immigration to Pennsylvania, 78.
SENECAS
Role in Grand Council, 24.
SHICKALLEMY (Swatane)
Participant in treaty councils, 48.
Iroquois envoy to border tribes, 48.
Personal sketch, 48.
Death of (1749), 49.
Friendship with Conrad Weiser, 53.
SHORT, William
Letter from Jefferson, 108.
SIX NATIONS (See also: Five Nations, Iroquois)
Strategic position vis-à-vis English, French, 42.
Cadwallader Colden among, 44.
At Lancaster treaty council (1744), 58, 59.
At Carlisle treaty council (1753), 66.
Meeting with united colonists (1775), 74.
Thanked for advice: Colonial union, 76.
Benjamin Franklin and, 83.
SMITH, W. S.
Letter from Jefferson, 113–114.
SPAIN
Source of immigration to New World, 35.
SPECK, Frank G.
Cited, 11–12.

Index

SQUANTO
Visits Europe, 4.
Greets Pilgrims in New World, 4, 34.
STAMP ACT
Colonists rally against, 75.
Benjamin Franklin's writings after, 96.
STANDING ARROW (Seneca)
And Edmund Wilson, 16, 19.
STANDING BEAR (Lakota)
Quoted, xi.
SUSQUEHANAH INDIANS
And Swedish missionary, 89–90.
SYRACUSE, New York
At site of Iroquoian Grand Council fire, 23.

THANKSGIVING
First feast, 4.
THOMAS, Gov. George, Esq.
Greets Iroquois at Lancaster treaty council (1744), 59.
Role at treaty council, 59.
Urges alliance with Iroquois, 59–60.
Response to Canassatego, 62.
TREATY COUNCILS (See also: individual councils)
Diplomatic significance, 47.
Proceedings widely read, 47.
Protocol at councils, 53–54.
As forums for ideas, 53.
Accounts published by Benjamin Franklin, 54.
TURNER, Frederick Jackson
"Frontier Hypothesis," 16.
TURTLE (Iroquois clan), 28.
TURTLE ISLAND
Iroquois name for North America, 30.
TUSCARORAS
Join Iroquois Confederacy, 21.
Lack voting rights in Grand Council
TWIGHTWEES (Indians)
Alliance with British and Iroquois, 67.
Attacked by French (1752), 67.

UNDERHILL, Ruth
Cited, 15.

UNITED NATIONS
Declaration of rights compared to Iroquois' Great Law of Peace, 17–18, 29, 123–124.
Indian nations petition, 123.
UNITED STATES
Mentioned, xii, 118.
Governmental structure compared to Iroquois', 9–10, 15, 17–18, 20.
Revolutionary ideology of founders, 54.
Federal governmental structure, 73–74.
Born during Enlightenment, 125.

VAN DOREN, Carl
Cited, 11.
Indian treaties printed by Benjamin Franklin, 62f.
VENANGO
French fort at, 67.
VIKINGS
Travel to America, 3–4.
VIRGINIA
Commissioners at Lancaster treaty council, 46, 58, 59, 85.
Iroquois influence on frontier of, 69.
VOLTAIRE, 14.
de VOTO, Bernard
Cited, 6.

WAITE, Robert
On Cadwallader Colden, 36.
WALLACE, Paul A. W.
Iroquois Confederacy compared to United Nations, 12, 15, 18.
Beginnings of Iroquois Confederacy, 22.
Indian governments resemble *Utopia*, 120.
WAMPUM
Belts as written communication, 28, 29.
Political significance, 26.
Great Law of Peace recorded on, 29.
Used to record contracts, 29.
Used to assist memory, 29.
Used as medium of exchange, 30.
Fabrication of, 30.
Diplomatic uses, 30.

[166]

Index

WASHINGTON, George
Mentioned, 15
Collects Indian grammars, 94.
Indian-warfare (guerilla) tactics, 117.
WRAXALL, Peter
Reproves William Johnson for sexual exploits, 51.
WEISER, Conrad
Mentioned, 78.
Adopted by Iroquois, 52, 58.
Participant in treaty councils, 47.
Personal sketch, 52.
And Lancaster treaty, 85.
Supplies Benjamin Franklin with treaty accounts, 52, 57–58.
Friendship with Canassatego, 52, 88, 90.
Hosts Iroquois at Lancaster treaty council (1744), 52, 58–59.
Friendship with Shickallemy, 53.
Friendship with Benjamin Franklin, 58.

Delivers Lancaster treaty council account to Benjamin Franklin, 58.
Meets Canassatego at Lancaster (1744), 58.
Recalled by Benjamin Franklin, 88.
WHEELOCK, Matthew, 77, 100.
WILD POTATOES (Iroquois clan), 28.
WILLIAM AND MARY (College), 85.
WILLIAMSBURG, Virginia
Site of William and Mary College, 85.
Jefferson plans trip to (1776), 100.
WILSON, Edmund
Cited, 16, 19.
WISSLER, Clark
"Iroquois family," 45.

ZOLLA, Elemire
Cited, 18–19.

[167]